D0872625

opening moves:

John Keegan

august 1914

WITHDRAWN

Editor-in-Chief: Barrie Pitt
Editor: David Mason
Art Director: Sarah Kingham
Picture Editor: Robert Hunt
Designer: David A Evans
Cover: Denis Piper
Special Drawings: John Batchelor
Photographic Research: Benedict Shephard
Cartographer: Richard Natkiel

First Printing: August 1971
Printed in United States of America

Ballantine Books Inc.
101 Fifth Avenue New York NY 10003

An Intext Publisher

Contents

Drama never surpassed

Introduction by Barrie Pitt

To European minds, World War I – the Great War as we call it – stretches across time like a curtain; beyond it is history, this side is the world we live in. The strands of the life we live today can be traced backwards through the sixties with comparative ease, through the fifties and forties – a few tangles in the early forties but these can be quite easily unsnarled – clearly from this distance through the thirties (though God knows, life was bewildering enough at the time) on through the pale and diminishing twenties as far as the end of 1918. There the strands end. They have reached the curtain – the Great War, the most prodigious historical event since the followers of Mahomet carved an empire from Cordova to the gates of Samarkand.

Dimly beyond this curtain can be perceived a life which seems to bear no relation to the present one, conducted apparently to a different rhythm, by a different species of being, reacting to a totally different scheme of behaviour. Bewhiskered monarchs write stiff family notes to each other before going out to shoot stag or bird, tiara'd queens whisper behind their fans, frock-coated statesmen hurry from capital to capital and debate in solemn conclave (occasionally one is shot), while the tight-collared and cloth-capped masses alternately riot or cheer, fortified the while on ale, wine, or porter at a penny a pint. Away in a far corner a square of British infantry in blue and scarlet repels cavalry charges or hordes of fanatical natives: perhaps the most astonishing aspect of the world beyond the curtain is that the sun seems to have been shining all the time. No wonder we feel so sense of heredity towards it.

Yet that world was the precursor of this one; emotion and intellect are deadlocked. Whatever else the Great War might have produced, it rang no changes in the reproductive system and we cannot evade the realization that the world beyond that curtain was peopled by our grandfathers and great-grandfathers. The actual kinship therefore is direct and close. What broke the

sense of continuity, the drift of time? An event, obviously of cataclysmic proportions. As such, it attracts the attention of anyone who happens to glance over his shoulder, with some of the compulsion of the view from Enola Gay as she sped away from Hiroshima on the morning of the 6th August, 1945.

The simile is purposely chosen. A hundred accounts of that particular event have been read with fascinated horror ever since; the same root fascination encompasses the Great War – and no part of the Great War compares in interest with its opening.

It is not too much to say that the first thirty days of battle determined the future course of the war, the terms of the peace and the shape of the world and all its nations since that time. The battles of August 1914 are now a part of European legend and the names of Liege, Mons, Charleroi, Guise and Rossignol are emblazoned on the battle honours of some of Europe's most famous regiments.

The German sweep to the Marne through the torrid heat of that cataclysmic month was one of the greatest parades of military strength the world has ever seen – and the amazing recovery of the shattered and disorganised French army which enabled them first to hold and then to throw back the German armies from the Marne was indeed the miracle it was named at the time.

John Keegan tells this story in the pages which follow with the same lucidity which distinguishes his previous books in this series, *Barbarossa* and *Waffen SS*, marshalling his facts with the integrity we have come to expect from this distinguished historian. He has written a superb account of what Winston Churchill was to call 'a drama never surpassed' . . . all that happened afterwards consisting in battles which, however formidable and devastating, were but desperate and vain appeals against the decisions of Fate.

War plans

The creation of the German Empire, which was proclaimed in the Hall of Mirrors at Versailles in 1871, marked the culmination and triumph of Bismarck's German policy. For the first time since the middle ages, the majority of the German- speaking peoples of Europe would henceforth belong to a single state; for the first time in history, that state would be almost exclusively German-speaking. From a nationalist, or as a nationalist would have said, from a *völkisch* point of view, the boundaries of the new Empire excluded rather too many Germans to be accepted with complete enthusiasm. But Bismarck had always set his face against including the Germans of Austria, not wanting their Habsburg masters to claim title to the new Imperial throne, and as for the Germans of the south and east, all those expatriate communities living somewhere between 'the Meuse and the Memel, the Belt and the Echt' only a German nationalist of the most extreme hue could look forward to a time when they should be gathered into the Reich.

But, great though Bismarck's political achievement was, its diplomatic and more important its strategic implications were fraught with uncertainty and danger for Germany. For the new Reich, through

The Proclamation of Wilhelm I as German Emperor, Versailles, 1871

its inheritance of Prussia's Polish possessions and through its annexation of the French provinces of Alsace and Lorraine, was to acquire two neighbours of daunting military power: to the east, Russia, to the west, France. France, whose acceptance of defeat in the war of 1870-71 was to follow swiftly on that proclamation in the Hall of Mirrors, could be counted for the future an implacable foe. Russia, though having had no quarrel with any German state for sixty years, and though having taken no part in the settlement of the 'German question', clearly could not favour the emergence of a second great Central European power to take its place besides Austria. Given their common anxieties about her, Germany must regard Russia and France as potentially disposed to ally against her. And it would become in conse-quence the principal and paramount aim of Bismarck's diplomacy to keep them apart. By many means, but principally by the famous Reinsurance Treaty which secured 'the neutrality of Russia in a war provoked by France by promising neutrality to Russia in a war provoked by Austria', he could assure himself, by the end of the 1880s, that he had made the future safe for Germany.

It was a safety which ultimately depended, of course, on the possession of armed force but Moltke, Bismarck's great military colleague, shared his belief in the need to avoid war on two fronts. He also shared Bismarck's belief in moderation. Should war on two fronts break out, Moltke planned to contain the situation by acting

9

Above : The French Army in rout, Sedan, 1870   *Below :* The Battlefield of Sedan, 1870

defensively until one enemy or the other grew tired and sued for peace or, an unlikely outcome, exposed itself to a crippling blow. He did not intend to attempt a decisive offensive in any other circumstances. Both Moltke and Bismarck knew the risk and strain that aggressive policies entailed, since they had won German unification by such policies in the 1860s. They intended that neither they nor their successors should face, or expose Germany to, such risks again.

The first Kaiser was of a mind with them. His death in 1888, however, brought to the throne a young man, his grandson Wilhelm II, who took the opposite view. He craved a more 'adventurous' foreign policy, meaning a more provocative and so more dangerous one, conceived a passion to possess a large navy, which was bound to unsettle relations with Britain, and permitted the army, under its new Chief of Staff, Count Alfred von Schlieffen, to prepare plans for an offensive, instead of defensive,

solution to the two-front war problem.

Schlieffen, who after a brief interval succeeded Moltke in 1891, was as different from him in outlook and capacity as the new Chancellor Caprivi was from Bismarck, who he succeeded, or the young from the old Kaiser. Moltke had proved himself in two campaigns and on half a dozen major battlefields a supreme practitioner of the craft of war, and of modern, steam-age war at that; at the same time demonstrating that, over and above that craft, he placed the art of politics. His relations with Bismarck had always been informed by the warmest and most intelligent mutual regard, as his war plans had conformed with and meshed into Bismarck's diplomatic designs. Schlieffen lacked Moltke's advantages. He has never exercised high command in the field nor had he seen politics from the inside. He was that peculiarly late 19th century creature, the professional staff officer.

Britain and America, whose small, amateurish armies were shielded from the responsibility of guaranteeing the national security by broad tracts of sea, did not produce that type. France, Austria, and above all Germany, produced him in numbers. Ironically they did so under the influence, direct and indirect, of Helmuth von Moltke. For it was he who, as Chief of the German Great General Staff, had demonstrated the primary importance of good staff work in warfare and previously as director of the Berlin *Kriegsakademie* (on which all staff colleges were subsequently to be modelled) had ensured that Germany should, at a decisive moment, have a monopoly of staff officers of the right sort.

The right sort meant, in Moltke's view, men who had been trained in a common doctrine of war and a common routine of work, this in turn ensuring that in a crisis all headquarters could continue to work cooperatively even if temporarily out of touch with each other. It was an ideal

Bismarck

Kaiser Wilhelm II

Kaiser Wilhelm I

Moltke the Elder

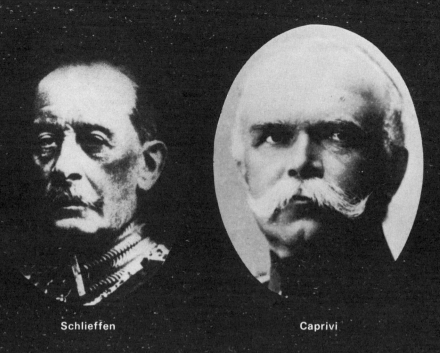

Schlieffen   Caprivi

Bismarck dictating the terms of peace to Favre and Thiers, 1871

Clausewitz

gerate the rôle that doctrine and routine would play in the work, and, above all, in the operational planning of the Great General Staff. What had been created to serve a master mind was now to become the 'brain of the army'.

Unfortunately, it was a brain of rigid patterns of thought and limited outlook. Moltke's wars, like those of Napoleon, whose disciple he acknowledged himself to be, had been short and decisive. The aim in each of them had been, as Clausewitz, the great Prussian interpreter of Napoleon, had laid down, the destruction of the enemy's field army. The methods had been those which Clausewitz had prescribed (had invested indeed with a sort of moral imperative): the rapid concentration of overwhelming mass at a critical point (*Schwerpunkt*), a surprise attack, an unrelenting pursuit. Concentration, mass, surprise, manoeuvre, pursuit, and a speedy decision. These were the golden rules of Moltkean warfare. And when applied by Moltke, working in concert with Bismarck, they had won legendary victories and ample political advantage for Prussia.

Bequeathed to the Great General Staff, these golden rules, which Moltke had occasionally been prepared to break, and had always seen merely as means, became sanctified. Doctrine became dogma. Victory, which Moltke had used as a stepping stone to peace, became an end in itself. Nothing demonstrated this more clearly than Schlieffen's approach to the two-front war problem.

The *Aufmarsch* (deployment) plan which Schlieffen inherited foresaw Germany, in the event of a two-front war, making her major effort on the eastern front in concert with Austria, while awaiting a French attack in the west. For a time Schlieffen tinkered with it, but never enthusiastically. He disapproved (in one of his rare political judgements) of Germany's involvement with Austria, since without it he believed Germany and

which demanded a long and rigorous training of the most carefully selected officers, and thereafter their sequestration from the mainstream of army life. Trained staff officers were of course required to return to regimental duty at regular intervals, in order to refresh their memories of the problems of service at that level, but admission to the Great General Staff, towards which every *Kriegsakademie* candidate strove, meant in effect election to a ruling circle. And because it ruled in a very real sense – the Great General Staff Officer had the right to register his protest if a commander rejected his advice, thus giving him an effective veto over decisions – the natural tendency of the Great General Staff and its members (less than a thousand in number) was to grow away from the mass of the army. That had never been Moltke's intention and as long as he stood at its head, as he did for thirty years, he restrained it. His departure did not merely remove that check. In making room for a successor whose upbringing had been almost completely theoretical, it served to exag-

Russia could live at peace; but he disapproved even more strongly of the indecisive objects the campaigns envisaged. From August 1892 onwards, he began to explore, with increasing intensity as time drew on, the alternative of an initial attack against France which would have *decisive results*.

To telescope this process, his reasoning was as follows: the Russian army was large – too large for Germany to destroy in a single blow or to encircle quickly, even with the help of the Austrian army; but if the campaign in the east was not ended at a single blow, it would drag on, with fatal results, for the geography of the land would permit, in fact encourage, the Russians to fight an interminable series of delaying actions, each of which would draw the Germans deeper into the steppe, lengthening their lines of communication and weakening them for the kill. The Germans, in short, would suffer the fate that Napoleon's Great Army had under-

gone a century earlier and Charles XII's a century before that.

But, if Russia's army was so large and powerful, how could Schlieffen risk leaving it in his rear if and when he led the mass of the German army westward against France? The answer, in part, was that Germany's eastern frontier was well fortified (as was Russia's: another reason to avoid attacking her) but, more important, that the Russian army was known to be much slower to mobilise than the French. That was due both to the very much greater distances that Russian reservists had to travel to reach their mobilisation centres and to the comparatively sparse Russian railway network, but above all to the dilatoriness of Russian bureaucracy, both military and civilian. The advantage of time that Germany would gain therefrom over the Russians was difficult to estimate: certainly a

A Russian rifle company in service dress, 1914

Russian infantry on the line of march 1914

month, possibly six weeks. Since Germany herself would take a fortnight to mobilise, victory must be achieved within the succeeding four weeks. The eastern frontier could not safely be left unguarded any longer than that, allowing for the time it would take to extricate sizeable forces from France and rail them back through Germany.

This short space of time seemed to Schlieffen insufficient to achieve anything decisive against France, at least in his preliminary studies. The common Franco-German frontier, which stretched from Luxembourg to Switzerland, was only 150 miles long and fortifications, to which the mountains of the Vosges and the Côtes du Meuse, at the southern and northern ends respectively, lent considerable natural strength, reduced the 'effective operational length' of the frontier to forty miles. And this unfortified gap (the Trouée de Charmes) was a deliberate omission by the French, designed to serve as the mouth of a sausage machine. Schlieffen had no intention of permitting the German army to enter it. But if the French did not come forward from their fortresses – 'a kindly favour which we cannot count on them doing us' – how was he to get at them?

By 1897 (four years after France and Russia had signed a secret formal alliance, a secret at which Germany guessed) Schlieffen had found the nerve to articulate the obvious military (if politically unthinkable) answer: he could get at them through Belgium. That state, by an international treaty of 1839 to which France, Britain and Germany (as heir to Prussia's responsibilities) were signatories, was deemed permanently neutral and to violate her neutrality would be to commit the gravest offence in international law. But the growing spectre of 'encirclement' seemed to justify to Schlieffen,

as it would to many Germans, breaking paper laws in order to honour the law of self-preservation. By 1905, the year before his retirement, Schlieffen had arrived at the ultimate in the violation of Belgian neutrality. He planned to sweep as far north as Antwerp (by a violation also of Dutch neutrality from which his successor shrank), and then, wheeling right past Lille, to approach the French capital directly from the north. His balance of force in this manoeuvre would allot over three times as much to the right as to the left, which would face the French fortified area. The object of so lop-sided a deployment was twofold, first, to overcome very quickly the great Belgian fortresses on the Meuse, which blocked access to the bridges into northern France, second, and more important, to deliver a blow of devastating weight against the French left. The battle which would ensue when that encounter occurred was to begin with a strategic envelopment

and end with a total annihilation of the French army. It would come about the quicker if the French did him the favour of attacking towards the Rhine: but even if they did not, he believed that his plan would take them so unawares and off-balance that they would not be able to recover.

The only blemish on the paper perfection of his plan was provided by Paris. For Paris, the 'city of light' to the nineteenth-century world and an image of cultural energy and civilised ease to us, had another face: that of a fortress, the greatest fortress in Europe. In 1914, it was still enclosed by walls, which the broken armies of Napoleon III had defended against the Prussians in 1870-71; it was protected by outlying artillery redoubts and permanently garrisoned by 100,000 soldiers. Hence, it could not be taken without the expenditure of much trouble and time, as the Germans had found once before; but if left untaken, its garrison would pose a deadly threat to the flank or rear of

Above: German Uhlans defile on manoeuvres   Below: Falkenhayn (2nd from left, front row), the Kaiser, Moltke the younger, at the Kaiser manoeuvres, 1913
Below right: A German infantry battalion in column of companies, 1914

The Kaiser rides with his Footguards through Berlin, 1914

any army operating in its vicinity.

How was that threat to be overcome? Clearly in one of two ways: either by using the right-hand German army to mask Paris, in which case its neighbours would be left to fight the French in a purely frontal engagement, an unsatisfactory solution since it could not lead to a speedy decision and might lead to no decision at all; or else by bringing up extra corps to invest Paris, thus leaving the right-hand army free to envelop the French left wing. Unfortunately, this second solution proved, after careful calculation, an operational impossibility. Even if the army were to wring from the Reichstag sufficient funds to raise the necessary additional corps (seven would be needed) Schlieffen could find no space to accommodate them on his route maps. Every bit of the French road system would already be crammed with the columns of the field armies. Hence, in wistful judgement, he concluded in his final testamentary exposition: 'the Germans will be brought to realise that they are too weak for the enterprise they have undertaken.' 'We shall find the experience of all earlier conquerors confirmed, that a war of aggression calls for much strength and also consumes much, that this strength dwindles constantly while the defender's increases.' Prophetic words.

Thus, the Schlieffen plan may be seen as unsatisfactory on three counts: it was a purely military plan, the product of a military contemplative's hours of solitude in his map room; it was a fatally inflexible plan, since it committed Germany in any military crisis to an attack on France, whether or not France had thrown down the challenge; and it was a plan which, for all it seemed to promise, would not work, by its creator's own admission. Poor recommendation for accepting it as the basis of Germany's war strategy. Yet so his successors did, translating its broad requirements into detailed rail movement

Joffre

tables and precise itineraries which, year by year, until 1914 were scrupulously kept up to date. No alternative plan was prepared, so that when, as we shall see, the Kaiser, on the night of 1st August, asked his Chief of Staff whether they could not direct the army eastward, he was told that it was quite impossible: the movement tables for such a shift of plan did not exist.

The history of the Schlieffen plan is an illustration of one way in which the 'pure staff mind' could distort the rational development of a national strategy. We may call it the way of intellectual distortion. Almost simultaneously, the activity of 'pure staff minds' in France was effecting another form of distortion on *her* strategy. We may call it philosophical distortion. This is its history.

Schlieffen, for all his 'staff mind' was no fool. The great envelopment he had planned was made necessary, in his view, not merely by Germany's peculiar strategic situation, but also by the nature of modern war, which rendered frontal attacks colossally costly, and tended always towards stalemate, static operations and siege.

The French General Staff, which was prepared to take the credit for having adopted the most effective quick firing cannon yet issued to any artillery, did not take Schlieffen's view. Despite the volume of firepower which it was known their own army could deliver, its officers had been led to believe, under the tutelage of Professor Foch of the *Ecole Supérieure* that the headlong offensive was still, indeed was now more than ever, the decisive method in warfare, that moral qualities counted for more than material power and that victory would go to he who would not believe that he had been beaten.

This philosophy of offensive war did not develop in France until several years past the turn of the century. Originally, French strategic thinking had been distinctly defensive, as the deep belt of fortifications on her eastern frontier testified. Since its completion, however, French war planning had grown more and more offensive, culminating in 1912 in the promulgation of Plan XVII. It had been written in reaction to the ideas of a fallen Commander-in-Chief designate, General Michel, who had argued that the by now traditional French scheme of deploying behind the Franco-German frontier provided no defence against the danger of a German invasion via Belgium. Unfortunately, he linked his proposals for a redeployment in that direction with others for the re-organisation of the army, which proved unpopular, and in the ensuing conflict in the War Council he and both his schemes were dismissed. In his place the French government put Joseph Joffre, a compromise candidate but even so an unlikely choice. Enormous in girth and disconcertingly silent, he was by training a sapper and by background a colonial soldier. In the British army such a combination of qualities was quite common and not necessarily a bar to advancement, as the careers of Gordon and Kitchener could show. But colonial service was a backwater

for a French officer and the engineers not a corps from which generals were frequently chosen. If the two obvious competitors for the succession, Pau and Galliéni, had not respectively withdrawn and demanded unacceptable terms, Joffre would not have been considered. When he was, his less obvious qualities commended him. He was an organiser of ability, well known for his equable temperament. He was Republican. But he was not anti-clerical.

These last considerations require explanation. France was a country, quite unlike militaristic Germany, in which government and army were at odds, the substance of their disagreement being over the status of the Church. Radical governments had, since the 1890s, set themselves to reduce both the property and the influence of the Church, in this latter respect by seeking to fill official posts of every sort with 'anti-clericals'. The army, which recruited its officers from those upper and middle class families which kept up their practice of religion, remained the only body sufficiently powerful to resist the anti-clerical campaign. In consequence, the government chose to doubt its 'Republicanism' and sought to ensure that it should not be commanded by officers from the Catholic camp. The conflict was at heart a ritualistic affair, for the army had no desire or intention to overthrow the state or even intervene in politics, just as the government entertained no real hope of 'republicanising' the officer corps. But the conflict was also real enough to take a nasty turn at times, as over the dual affairs of Dreyfus and the tribunals. The army had probably made a scapegoat of the former, who was regarded as 'Republican' because his Jewishness meant that he could not be counted among the Catholics; the tribunals had punished officers by witholding promotion from them only because they were Catholic.

Hence the suitability of Joffre. He

had friends on both sides of the quarrel and enemies on neither. Unfortunately, in the purely military field, he did not as yet have a mind of his own and in the ensuing two years (he was appointed on 28th July 1912) he allowed himself to be over-influenced by advisers in both strategy and tactics. Tactically, he was brought to endorse the ideas of the young school of staff officers, who would substitute for all forms of manoeuvre and supporting fire the direct or precipitate assault. Strategically, he was led to adopt Plan XVII, which embodied a strident rejection of Michel's analysis of the situation and a whole-hearted reversion to the deployment concept of earlier schemes. By its provisions, the French were to form up in five armies, four arrayed in line from Sedan to Belfort, with the weight in the centre opposite Metz, and the Fifth Army aligned behind the centre in reserve. As soon as concentration was complete, the armies were to attack eastward along two major thrust lines, one leading towards the Rhine via the Lorraine gateway, the other towards Metz. Diversionary attacks, also frontal in character, were to be launched in the intervening gap. Aims and objectives were unspecified. It was implied that method – the attack itself, pushed fearlessly and relentlessly forward – would achieve victory.

Joffre seemed an unlikely commander to whom to entrust so whirlwind an enterprise. His figure and his manner spoke deliberation, caution, ponderousness. Still, he clearly possessed nerve. That might turn the trick.

The character of the German Chief of Staff, Helmuth von Moltke the younger, nephew of the great general, lacked Joffre's reassuring solidity. He possessed, besides his famous name, undoubted intelligence, but he directed it more readily into artistic

than military channels. He 'preferred to read philosophy, to play the 'cello and to translate Maeterlinck's *Péleas et Mélisande* to sharing the company of staff officers.' As we have seen, he

Moltke the Younger

undertook no real review of the Schlieffen plan, though by 1914 he had had eight years in which to do so, and he remained uncertain of his fitness to implement it in war. 'I do not know how I shall manage in the event of a campaign,' he had confessed in 1906, 'I am very self-critical.' He was also physically unfit and growing old; in 1914 he was sixty-six (Joffre was sixty-two). He was to be excellently served by subordinates. Germany, having invented the modern staff system, had maintained the highest standard of staff-training and staff work and OHL (*Oberste Heereslei- tung*), the field headquarters, could be counted on to work with superb efficiency under pressure. But im- peccable staff work was no longer a German monopoly. French GQG (Grand Quartier-General) was also staffed by officers of brilliance and dedication, and organised on lines which closely approximated to the German model. In a contest between the two, it would be the quality of command which would count, com- mand and communications. In both the French would, if war came, enjoy the advantage.

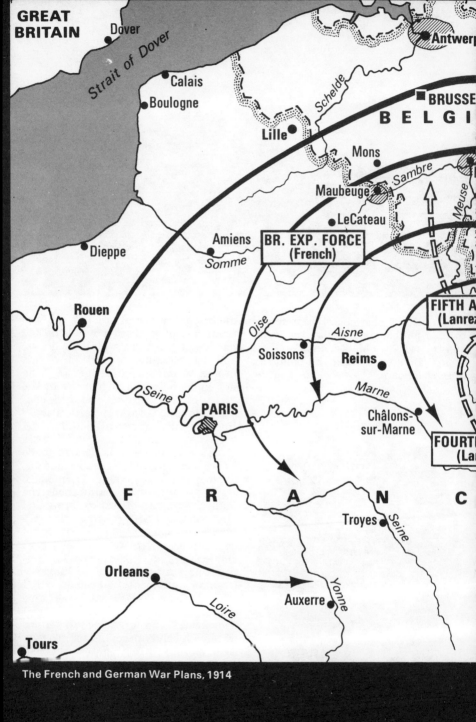

The French and German War Plans, 1914

Mobilisation and outbreak

If the general staffs of the major armies of Europe had increasingly turned in on themselves during the last years of the 19th century, yet at the same time army life and military service had tended more and more to become the common experience of every citizen. Conscription had been the basis on which European armies had been raised since the days of Napoleon (and a good deal earlier than that in Prussia). But conscription as a genuinely universal system had come into fashion only since the beginning of the 1870s, after the Prussian wars against Austria and France, which had demonstrated so compellingly the advantage which numbers conferred in modern warfare. For though both the Austrian and French armies which Prussia had defeated so summarily had been nominally conscript, in reality their soldiers had been long-service regulars, drafted by a form of lottery (in which the better-off could cheat by paying a substitute to take their place should they draw a 'bad' number). It was in short a peculiarly unfair system of selective service. And both the states which practised it were to pay a severe penalty for the civic injustice they inflicted thereby on their poorer citizens. For the disadvantage under which any long service army labours is the difficulty it has in accumulating large reserves, its 'throughput' of recruits being relatively slower than that of a short service army which, raised by universal conscription, will have a much higher turnover of manpower and hence much larger trained reserves to reinforce the Active army in time of war – as the Prussians showed in 1866 and 1870.

Europe took the point. After 1871 all major continental armies adopted universal short-service conscription as the basis of their military systems, with effects on the life-pattern of the able-bodied male population which varied little from country to country. Since the German system served as a model for all, its details provide a convenient explanation.

The young German registered for service at seventeen and was enrolled in what was called the 1st Ban of the *Landsturm;* from it, when his annual class reached the age of twenty, would be drawn sufficient men to fill the contingent which the Reichstag had voted funds to maintain for that year (as the result of a major piece of bargaining between the general staff and the ruling party). For the next two years his class served in the Active army (of which the officers and NCOs were of course regulars); if detailed to the cavalry or artillery he would serve three years – horsemastership and gunnery entailing a longer training. On completing his full-time service, he returned to civil life but was entered on the roll of the Reserve and recalled annually for short periods of training. At twenty-seven he passed from the Reserve to the *Landwehr*, another reserve the units of which would play a second-line rôle in the event of war; and at forty, he passed in to the 2nd Ban of the *Landsturm*, whose combatant function was nominal. At each turn, he would have been assigned to a unit whose depot was the closest to his dwelling place, so that in the event of mobilisation he could be embodied and kitted-out with the least possible delay. This 'localisation' policy had the added advantage of reinforcing regimental with local loyalties.

Local regiments were combined for administrative and tactical purposes to form brigades, brigades to form divisions and divisions to form corps; a corps area was designated a Military District and its borders usually coincided with those of a province. Thus, for example, the German VII Corps recruited and was based in Westphalia. Its two divisions, the 13th and 14th, had their headquarters respectively at Münster and Dusseldorf and the eight component infantry regiments were stationed each in another major provincial town, as

Above : German recruits in training, August 1914
Below : German recruits at bayonet drill

Above : Arms drill at a Frankfurt barracks, 1914
Below : Scaling a chevaux de frise

Above: German recruits at musketry training, 1914
Below: Riflemen (10th Hanoverian Jäger Battalion) in an outpost line, 1914

were the corps and divisional artillery regiments (cavalry was organised separately). In the event of mobilisation all these Active units of the corps would call in their quotas of reservists and complete to war strength. Supernumery reservists would then be formed up in fresh units, each the counterpart of an Active unit and officered by a special cadre of regulars, which when assembled would form the VII Reserve Corps (13th and 14th Reserve Divisions). Besides this, the Corps District would also yield eight *Landwehr* regiments, a number of *Landsturm* battalions and, in all probability, a quota of *Ersatz* (replacement) battalions of young reservists surplus to the establishment both of the Active and Reserve Corps; in August 1914, VII Corps District was in fact to produce five *Ersatz* battalions and another thirty-six Reserve or mobile *Landwehr* battalions, besides the twenty-four in the Active divisions. This almost tripled Westphalia's normal contribution in manpower to the national defence; and such indeed would be the effect of mobilisation all over German. In terms of quantity, mobilisation increased the number of men under arms in Germany from 800,000 to 5,000,000, the size of the field army from 700,000 to 2,200,000 and the number of divisions from fifty-one to eighty-two.

Since it was in divisions that a nation's fighting strength was conventionally reckoned, it is worth describing exactly in what this formation consisted. Its bulk was infantry, twelve battalions, each a thousand strong, organised into four regiments. Two regiments (six battalions) formed a brigade – a tactical unit whose existence made for easier command in action. To support the infantry, the division included four regiments of field artillery, each of three six-gun batteries of 77mm field guns or field howitzers – making seventy-two pieces in all – to which must be added heavier artillery controlled at corps. Corps also allotted each of its divisions a share of a cavalry and an engineer regiment.

France counted fewer divisions in her order of battle than Germany, forty-eight Active instead of fifty-one, and twenty-five Reserve against thirty-one. Moreover she was able to raise as many as these only by the most prodigious efforts. The French population being both smaller and comparatively older than the German, her government was forced to conscript 82 per cent of each annual class as against 51 per cent in Germany and, from 1912 onwards, to retain all conscripts for three years full time service. Curiously, however, the French artificially limited the increase they might have effected in the size of their field army on mobilisation because of the prevailing general staff attitude to reserves. That attitude was that all but the youngest classes of reservists would take too long to bring up to acceptable standards of fitness and efficiency to make an increase in the number of reserve formations worthwhile. Nor was it thought useful to organise the reserve divisions into proper corps; instead they were to be formed into groups, which lacked most of the ancillary units necessary to large formations, particularly heavy artillery. But then, the French took a dismissive view of the usefulness of heavy artillery in general. Their active units were very deficient in guns of large calibre, excessive reliance being placed on the 'seventy-five' – the remarkably mobile and rapid-firing 75mm field gun which the French possessed in abundance. Its characteristics, unlike those of heavier pieces, accorded perfectly with the general staff's creed of the headlong offensive.

The two other great armies of Europe, the Russian and the Austrian, approximated more or less in their organisation to the German pattern. Both however were beset by peculiar problems. Austria's was that of the

'Dual System' – German control of one half of the Empire, Hungarian of the other, which the Hungarians had insisted should be extended to the army. In consequence, while the Empire ran an Imperial or so-called Joint Army, equivalent to the Active army in France or Germany, it was also forced to allow the Hungarians an army of their own and, to match it, had to maintain a similar force in the German half. These two bodies, the *Honved* and *Landwehr*, which may in some sense be compared with the National Guards of the American states, performed something of the rôle of the reserve in other armies, but less efficiently and at greater cost. Austria's mobilised strength was consonantly lower than that of a state of comparative size. Her equipment, too, was often inferior and the contingents raised among the 'nationalities' – the half dozen races of the Empire not German or Hungarian – were of doubtful trustworthiness.

Russia's problem was an *excess* of

Watching the soldiers leave, Vienna, July 1914

numbers. Neither her bureaucracy nor her revenue could support the effort of conscripting all her male subjects who came of military age each year and in practice she called up only thirty-one per cent of the class. Even so, this percentage was sufficient to provide her with a peacetime army of seventy-nine divisions of infantry and the enormous total of twenty-four divisions of cavalry, including Cossacks. On mobilisation she would raise thirty-five reserve divisions but many would have to be transported so far to the concentration areas that they could not be counted in the initial order of battle. Unlike other armies, therefore, Russia kept a high proportion of her Active divisions in or near the concentration areas on her European frontier, which they would have to defend while mobilisation proceeded. Even when completed, Russia would be com-

A foretaste of trench warfare

Above: Answering the mobilisation order, Berlin, 1914
Right: The first British volunteers, Lincolnshire

paratively weaker than Germany for her trained reserves, relative to the size of her army, were fewer. An enormous militia, the *Opolchenie*, existed to provide replacements but few of its millions had received training.

The minor armies of Europe which the war would embroil – the Belgian, Serbian and Montenegrin – approximated in varying degree to the common pattern. There was one important exception: the British army. For Britain, alone among European powers, clung to the pre-Napoleonic tradition of voluntary service. This she could afford to do because her frontiers were guaranteed by the Royal Navy and because her Empire could be largely protected by local levies – or by the magnificent Indian (native) army. Her traditions, moreover, both constitutional and strategic, were against maintaining a large army at home. On the one hand, the name of Cromwell raised unpleasant memories of military rule; on the

other, the history of her army seemed to demonstrate that diversionary warfare conducted by amphibious expeditions had always won greater success than major continental campaigns (which one could usually subsidise an ally to wage). Hence Britain planned, in the event of war with Germany (a contingency her general staff had been discussing with the French since 1906), to intervene initially with only six divisions. But even that would almost denude the country of troops. For behind the regulars, all seven-year service men, stood the scantiest of trained reserves, and to supplement these there were only the Territorials, a citizen volunteer militia whose longest annual period of training was a fortnight. Little wonder that when Bismarck was asked what he would do if the

British landed on the Frisian coast, his answer had been, 'Send for the police'. But as the Germans were to find, the British regular army was of a fighting worth quite out of proportion to its numbers. Like the white colonial units of the French army, which were to perform so brilliantly in the Battle of the Frontiers, the British infantry battalions contained a high proportion of officers and men with active service experience. Unlike the French, they also set much store by good marksmanship, and could shoot the average conscript unit off the face of a battlefield. (In August 1914 the 2nd Bedfords were to engage German infantry near Mons at a range of 900 yards and drive them away.)

An advantage of the small scale of the British army – and of distances within the islands – was that mobilisation was a quick and simple procedure. Personal telegrams sufficed to summon all reservists to their depots within twenty-four hours. The same method brought in naval reservists to the fleet (which by a combination of chance and foresight was to be practising mobilisation at the moment of outbreak in August 1914). The larger numbers in the continental reserves made their mobilisation very much more complicated and would have made it much more time-consuming had not a great deal of forethought been given to streamlining the process. The essence of quick mobilisation at the beginning of the 20th century lay in the efficient management of the railways (just as it was the development of railways which had made manpower in mass a realisable military asset). The Germans had first perfected rail mobilisation and had set up a railway section of the general staff, with power both to dictate the pattern of new construction in peace and to assume

Above: Naval reservists report at Portsmouth Below: Crowds outside Buckingham Palace, 4th August 1914 Right: 2nd Scots Guards leave the Tower of London for France

control of all running in war, some time ahead of the other European armies. After 1870, the others had naturally followed suit and by 1914 it would have been difficult to judge whether the German or French armies were more efficient at railway management. The Austrians, with a poorer railway system, would be slower to complete mobilisation, the Russians very much so. Their reservists had to travel on average 700 miles to reach their depots, the French or German reservist only fifty miles. As a result, the French planned to concentrate the first wave of Active divisions on the frontier on the fifth day from mobilisation, the rest by the ninth day and the reserve divisions between the eleventh and thirteenth days; the German time table was almost precisely similar. Both programmes demanded the monopolisation of the rail network and the employment of enormous quantities of transport: 20,000 trains in seventeen days in the case of the Germans. To cover the arrival of all these transports at the railheads, both armies kept what were known as 'covering' divisions permanently at war strength within the concentration areas and planned to detrain their cavalry divisions there within four days of mobilisation.

Clearly, once mobilisation had been decreed, it was bound to invest international disagreement with a strong element of drama and diplomatic exchanges with an unwelcome quality of urgency. The temptation to surrender either to panic or to a sense of helplessness would act powerfully on any statesman in such circumstances; the enormous scale and rapid pace of the mobilisation process might well make it seem to him irreversible. Indeed, it was commonly said before 1914 by people who should have known better that 'Mobilisation means war'. The facts did not support such a judgement. Austria had twice fully and twice partially mobilised in the decade before 1914 without precipita-

ting a general conflict. On the other hand, the causes had been local and their limited nature had been recognised by the powers. When men said 'Mobilisation means war', they alluded to simultaneous action by the four great powers, and they probably thought particularly of Germany, whose central situation invested her behaviour in an international crisis with crucial significance. Indeed, we can now see that as long as Germany abided by Schlieffen's intentions, her mobilisation certainly would mean war. For the success of the plan demanded its immediate implementation; any delay would erode the margin of time which Russia's tardiness granted. We can also see that, during the July crisis of 1914, mobilisation or the threat of mobilisation produced a crucial heightening of the tension on three occasions, Russia being to blame twice and Austria once, while it was German mobilisation which eventually precipitated the outbreak.

The course and motivation of the July crisis is well-known. It began on 28th June in the town of Sarajevo, capital of the province of Bosnia which Austria had annexed from Turkey, after a long interregnum, in 1908. The Bosnians, like so many of the subjects of the Habsburg Empire, were Slavs, Serbo-Croat by language and more strongly attracted in their loyalties to the independent Kingdom of Serbia than to the Emperor in Vienna. That loyalty was all the stronger for the comparatively recent re-emergence of an independent Serbian kingdom after five hundred years of subjection to Turkish rule and it was not therefore tactful of the Habsburg heir to have chosen the anniversary of the Turkish triumph over the Serbs in 1389 to pay Sarajevo a visit. Whether or not a slight had been intended it was felt, and a party of young Serbian nationalists had resolved on an attempt at assassination. Such was their ineptitude that it nearly failed, but unfortunately

Above: The Archduke Ferdinand and his wife at Sarajevo, 28th June 1914
Below: The Archduke and his wife in their car at Sarajevo

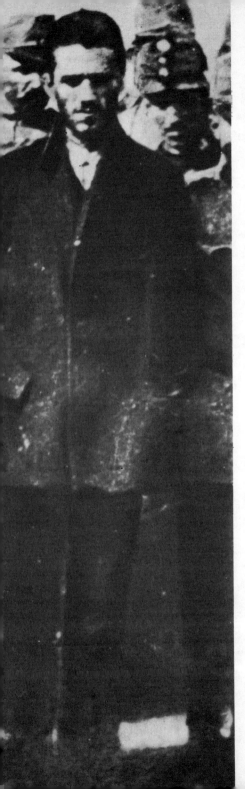

not quite. The assassin was captured and found under interrogation to be a Serb of Austrian nationality; the Vienna government decided nevertheless to accuse Serbia of complicity in the outrage and to present her with an ultimatum couched in terms so humiliating that she would be bound to choose hopeless military resistance rather than compliance.

Austria had long wished to crush Serbia. The Kingdom's independent existence threatened the viability of the Empire, not merely because it lent hope to the Emperor's disaffected Serb subjects but also because their disaffection could too easily infect all the other Slav minorities. If Vienna had refrained hitherto from embarking on a confrontation, it was because she had lacked a convincing pretext and, more important, the promise of German support in seeing the crisis through. The Sarajevo assassination and a change of heart in Berlin removed both those obstacles.

Berlin had always previously preached caution to Vienna in its Balkan policies, not wishing to see her embark on any policy which might lead to war with Russia, and so perhaps to a general European conflict. The change of attitude was due to a realisation that if Serbia was not reproved for the Sarajevo affair (whether or not her secret service had provoked the assassination), Austria's influence in the Balkans would be irretrievably damaged. Austria's loss of power would mean Russia's gain, and that Germany could not welcome; on the other hand, Russia was still recovering from her defeat in the war with Japan of 1904 and from the upheavals of 1905 and was probably still not prepared to fight. She would certainly protest and might threaten if Serbia were crushed but better that than await her return to strength in a spirit of good neighbourliness.

The Kaiser accordingly advised the

Princip, the Sarajevo assassin

Above: A Russian outpost, Manchuria, 1904
Below: A Japanese siege gun at Port Arthur 1904

Bethmann-Hollweg

Tisza

Austrian ambassador on 5th July to act against Serbia and the day following his Chancellor, Bethmann-Hollweg, gave his encouragement also. Their promise of support was quite specific: Germany would endorse Austria in any action she took against Serbia up to and including war. Given such a guarantee, and despite strong opposition from within the Imperial Crown Council, notably from the Hungarian Premier, Tisza, who warned that Russia would fight, the Austrian government decided to bring Serbia down.

There was a long delay in issuing the fatal ultimatum to Serbia. It did not appear until 23rd July. When it did, the ten demands embodied in it were recognised throughout Europe as being quite unacceptable, as they were intended to be. Austria, whose war plans envisaged two contingencies, a crisis in the Balkans calling for partial mobilisation (Plan B), and a general crisis calling for a mobilisation also against Russia (Plan R), ordered partial mobilisation in anticipation of a Serbian rejection of her terms. Serbia also mobilised on 25th

July but returned so conciliatory a reply at the end of the time limit that if events had continued to run a purely bilateral course it is difficult to see how Austria could have sustained her quarrel.

However, they did not. A chain reaction of European military measures had already been set in train, beginning in Russia. There, on 24th July, the Tsar had ordered the taking of certain precautionary measures and the implementation, to take effect on 26th July, of the 'Period Preparatory to War'. This pre-mobilisation procedure was one which had its counterpart in several European countries and was designed to put the Active army on a war footing without exacerbating a crisis; the equivalent procedure in Germany was the proclamation of the *Kriegsgefahrzustand*. Unfortunately, these measures, though amiably conceived in theory, were dangerously open to misinterpretation in practice.

Sazonov, the Russian foreign minister, had agreed to the implementation of the Period Preparatory to War on the understanding that it would not

Tsar Nicholas II

Sazonov

heighten tension. In particular, he expected the Austrians to accept that Russia's mobilisation of thirteen corps on their joint Carpathian frontier, the principal provision of the Period Preparatory, was no more than a formal retort to her partial mobilisation against Serbia and that she would accordingly not take countermeasures. When the head of the Russian mobilisation office pointed out to Sazonov that Austria would be compelled in self defence to proceed to full mobilisation, and that the terms of the Austro-German treaty probably bound the Germans to mobilise in sympathy, he did not, as he might, decide to defer implementing the Period Preparatory but decided instead to draft also a proclamation of general mobilisation. His intention was to lay both before the Tsar for signature and to decide later which he would implement in the light of the situation as it developed.

France meanwhile was experiencing a strong and growing sense of crisis. On 26th July, her government had ordered the recall of all troops from leave and, on the day following, the embarkation of the North African garrison, 100,000 strong. But its primary concern, and even more so that of the general staff, was with Russian intentions, the news of the partial mobilisation being extremely unsettling to men who had counted on an immediate Russian offensive into East Prussia to take the pressure off them in the event of a two-front war. Their views were strongly represented to the Tsar's government by the French Ambassador, Paléologue, who frankly exhorted Russia towards war in a most undiplomatic way throughout the crisis.

Sazonov, however, had still not made up his mind to proceed to general mobilisation as late as 29th July. On the morning of that day he received a telegram from Bethmann-Hollweg which, though described by the German ambassador who transmitted it as 'not a threat but a friendly warning', seemed to Sazonov both patronising and menacing. Its message was that 'further progress of Russian mobilisation measures would compel us to mobilise, and then European war could scarcely be pre-

Conrad von Hötzendorf

vented'. Sazonov's reaction to it was to advise the Tsar, after consulting the Chief of Staff, that 'the risk could not be accepted of delaying a general mobilisation'. Nicholas accordingly assented to the despatch of the necessary telegram.

At the last minute, the Tsar, whose wish for peace was genuine and profound, changed his mind and had the second telegram, ordering partial mobilisation, sent in its stead. It reached the four military districts at midnight on 29th July. But as the Russian general staff realised, news even of partial mobilisation would now, given the state of tension which had been generated, have the same effect as that of general mobilisation. Moltke, in Berlin, certainly took the view that by proceeding with partial mobilisation in the four western military districts Russia was stealing a march on Germany. He was particularly alarmed by the rumour that Conrad von Hötzendorf, the Austrian Chief of Staff, was planning after all to stand on the defensive in the Carpathians and on 30th June used his own channels of communication with

Vienna to urge Conrad to proceed at once to general mobilisation, thus, as he pointed out, automatically invoking German assistance.

In any case, the Russian general staff, aware that Germany and Austria might suddenly declare general mobilisation while the Russian army was moving towards partial mobilisation, and so catch it on the wrong foot, prevailed on the Tsar to order general mobilisation, to be proclaimed on 31st July. By accident, it was made public in St Petersburg on the evening of 30th July, but by then Moltke had persuaded the Kaiser that Germany's position would deteriorate vis-à-vis Russia and France unless military precautions were at once initiated. It was accordingly decided in the Crown Council to proclaim the *'drohende Kriegsgefahrzustand'* (state of imminent danger of war) on the following day, 31st July.

Austria, which had actually been at war with Serbia since 28th July, announced its own general mobilisation at the same time as the German government proclaimed the *Kriegsgefahrzustand*. The German general staff was now convinced that war could not be averted and was chiefly concerned that it should come about in circumstances which would conform most conveniently with their own plans: that is to say, that France and Russia should be brought into war against Germany simultaneously. Two ultimatums were accordingly drafted, both demanding the fulfilment of completely unacceptable conditions within a very short time limit. Russia was to cease mobilisation within twenty-four hours; France was within thirty-six hours to declare her neutrality and surrender for the duration of the crisis the frontier fortresses of Toul and Verdun.

France perfectly naturally rejected this ultimatum out of hand. Her covering troops had been deployed since 30th July, though ten kilometres short of the frontier, in order to avoid the risk of provocative

Above: The German 36th Regiment (V Corps) in field grey and full marching order
Below: Flowers in their buttonholes, the 4th Foot Guards leave Berlin

Above: Unter den Linden, 4th August, 1914. The portraits are of the Austrian and German Emperors
Below: German reservists ioining their regiment

Above: German reservists buckle on unfamiliar equipment. The infantryman of 1914 carried 60-70lbs on his body.
Below: The 7th Infantry Regiment leaves Bayreuth

ARMÉE DE TERRE ET ARMÉE DE MER

ORDRE
DE MOBILISATION GÉNÉRALE

Par décret du Président de la République, la mobilisation des armées de terre et de mer est ordonnée, ainsi que la réquisition des animaux, voitures et harnais nécessaires au complément de ces armées.

Le premier jour de la mobilisation est le dimanche deux août 1914

Tout Français soumis aux obligations militaires doit, sous peine d'être puni avec toute la rigueur des lois, obéir aux prescriptions du **FASCICULE DE MOBILISATION** (pages coloriées placées dans son livret).

Sont visés par le présent ordre **TOUS LES HOMMES** non présents sous les Drapeaux et appartenant :

1° à l'**ARMÉE DE TERRE** y compris les **TROUPES COLONIALES** et les hommes des **SERVICES AUXILIAIRES**;

2° à l'**ARMÉE DE MER** y compris les **INSCRITS MARITIMES** et les **ARMURIERS** de la **MARINE**.

Les Autorités civiles et militaires sont responsables de l'exécution du présent décret.

Le Ministre de la Guerre,   *Le Ministre de la Marine,*

Left: The French Mobilisation Poster
Above: Reservists entraining at the
Gare de l'Est, Paris

incidents. But on 31st July Joffre had
solemnly warned the French cabinet
that 'any delay of twenty-four hours
in calling up our reservists will have
as a result the withdrawal of our
concentration points from ten to
twelve miles for each day of delay;
in other words the initial abandon-
ment of just that much of our territory'. A mobilisation warning order,
in some sense the equivalent of the
Kriegsgefahrzustand had been issued
later the same day. On the morning
of 1st August Joffre advised the cabinet that mobilisation could be delayed with safety no longer and at
3.55pm the posters were pasted up in
the streets of Paris. Five minutes
later Germany announced her own
general mobilisation.

Britain remained the only major
European power which had as yet
made no overt military response to
the crisis. The fleet, which had been
practising one of its periodic trial
mobilisations, had been ordered to
refrain from dispersing on 29th July,
and the Admiralty had notified its
units of the inauguration of what was
known as the 'Precautionary Period'.

On 1st August, in response to urgent
French requests to safeguard the
Channel crossings, it ordered full
mobilisation. But the mobilisation of
a fleet never carries with it the same
threatening implication as that of an
army and the Cabinet was not yet
prepared to call up the army. Indeed
it was not until it had had firm news
of Germany's physical violation of
Belgian territory on 3rd August that
Grey, the Foreign Secretary, felt able
to reveal to the House of Commons
the existence of an understanding between the British and the French
general staffs and the thought the
government was giving to honouring
it. Later that day, the War Office made
public the general mobilisation order
and on 4th August Britain formally
announced the opening of hostilities
with Germany.

By then, the young manhood of
Europe in its millions had reported
to the regimental depots. Five great
armies were forming in France, eight
in Germany. One, the Eighth, was
concentrating in East Prussia, where
it was to bar Russia's path towards
Berlin. The other seven were moving
towards their allotted places on the
western frontier from which they
were to wheel forward towards Paris
and victory.

Above: Parisians cheer the news of mobilisation
Below: French Colonial Infantry at a Paris Station

Above: Flowers for Cuirassiers leaving Paris for the front
Below: The drums of a Zouave battalion on the way to war

Lorraine and the Ardennes

Plan XVII, which Joffre had inherited on assuming the post of Chief of Staff, committed the French army, immediately on completion of its mobilisation, to 'two major [offensive] operations, one on the right, in the country between the wooded district of the Vosges and the Moselle below Toul; the other, on the left, north of the line Verdun-Metz'. The first of these has come to be known as the Lorraine Offensive, the earliest phase of the Battle of the Frontiers. In Alsace, that battle was to have its beginning before even the preliminary stage of concentration was complete, as a result of the particularly intrusive 'covering' mission assigned to VII Corps. For while the other local frontier formations, XX Corps based at Nancy and XXI Corps at Epinal, had orders merely to take up positions from which they could protect the detraining areas of First and Second Armies, VII Corps, based at Besançon in the extreme south, was detailed by Joffre on 3rd August to set out immediately for Mulhouse, a town only a little short of the Rhine and deep in German-held territory, with the object at once of securing First Army's projected axis of advance and of raising the countryside against the enemy. Its commander, General Bonneau, prevaricated from the start and his subordinates seem to have caught his irresolution. He took two days to reach Mulhouse, a mere fifteen miles from his base, quite neglected to reconnoitre his front once arrived and lost the town within twenty-four hours of its capture to troops secretly assembled in the adjacent forests. By 11th August, he had beaten a retreat as far as Belfort, where he and the commander of his attacked cavalry division instantly received news of their dismissal.

Joffre had already found it necessary to remove one obviously incompetent

De Castelnau, with Joffre and Pau

Messimy

general. He was now to inaugurate a positive reign of terror over the French high command. 'My mind was fully made up on this subject', he wrote later. 'I would get rid of incapable generals and replace them with those who were younger and more energetic'. By the end of August the commander of one of the five armies, three of the twenty-one corps and thirty-six of the eighty-three divisions had been relieved; precisely equal numbers were dismissed in September. Messimy, the Minister of War, would have gone further, threatening death to any officer found wanting in courage or capacity. Joffre, who ruled absolute in the Zone of the Armies, suppressed that despatch. Rightly his concern was with efficiency, which he did not think would be served by barbaric threats, and it was for the same reason that he now began that refashioning of command structures which was to make his control of the fighting so much more positive than Moltke's throughout the campaign of 1914. He judged that much of Bonneau's vaccilation had been due to a lack of supervision of his actions. He accordingly separated VII Corps from First Army on 10th August and, by the addition of the 8th Cavalry Division, the 1st Group of (three) Reserve Divisions, several Alpine battalions and the 44th Division, the latter released by the dissolution of the Army of the Alps on Italy's declaration of neutrality, established round it a new Army of Alsace under General Pau.

These changes completed the deployment of the southern wing for the coming Battle of the Frontiers. North of the Army of Alsace and aligned along the crest of the Vosges stood the First Army, commanded by General Dubail, a man esteemed by Joffre for his mental toughness. His command, whose headquarters were located at the fortress town of Epinal, comprised the local XXI Corps, and VIII, XIII and XIV Corps, from the Alps and Centre. The Second Army, commanded from Nancy by General Castelnau, the 'Monk in Boots', so called for his ostentatious devotion to the Catholi

French dragoons marching to their concentration area

Church, disposed of a rather stronger force, as befitted its position astride the Charmes Trough: the local XX Corps, commanded by another devout believer, Ferdinand Foch (better known for his fervent advocacy of the offensive), the XV and XVI Corps from the Riviera and the IX and XVIII from Bordeaux and Touraine. Also subordinate were five reserve divisions and three of cavalry, shortly to be organised into a corps under General Conneau. The two armies, twenty-three divisions in all, were deployed on a comparatively narrow front of sixty-five miles between Pont à Mousson on the Moselle and St Marie-aux-Mines on the crest of the Vosges; the majority were in the Charmes Trough itself, only twenty-five miles wide.

Joffre issued his orders to the two armies on 8th August, in amplification of the general statement of intent contained in Plan XVII, which merely laid down that the southern wing had to mount an attack below Metz. His General Instruction No 1 directed

First Army 'to take as its objective the German army at Sarrebourg . . . and seek to put it out of action by driving it back on Strasbourg' aided by the Army of Alsace which, advancing through Belfort Gap via Mulhouse, was to wheel north-west along the Vosges and seize Colmar, destroying the Rhine bridges and securing the whole right wing from attack across the Rhine. Second Army, leaving its two left hand corps (IX and XVIII) to cover the approaches southwards from Metz, where the main body of the German army was supposed to lie, was to advance on Sarrbrucken, on the front Dieuze – Château Salins – Delme. These operations were to start as soon as the commanders were ready. Joffre issued his final instructions on 13th August, under a covering note to Dubail, in which he told him, 'I count on you absolutely for the success of this operation. It must succeed and

59

French infantry wait for the next German push forward

you must devote all your energy to it'.

Joffre's emphasis on the importance of these southern operations stemmed, of course, from his continual misunderstanding of the enemy's intentions and capabilities. Despite the appearance of German vanguards on the Belgian Meuse, he was still convinced that their main strength was drawn up in the centre; it consisted exclusively of Active corps, and he thought that they would use their strength to strike from Metz into Alsace-Lorraine. Joffre intended to pre-empt them by directing his first thrust to the Rhine. All of Joffre's presuppositions were unfounded, and though his misreading of Moltke's strategy was in the long term the gravest of all his mistakes, his failure to detect that the Germans had formed their Reserve divisions into first-line corps and were committing them to a front-line rôle was almost as serious. It boded very ill for First and Second Armies. As late as 16th August they were to be assured by GQG's Intelligence branch that they faced no more than six corps along their whole front, a comfortable balance in their favour.

Despite that assurance, neither First nor Second Army were to display much of that reckless offensive dash which legend associates with the Battle of the Frontiers. Their pace in the advance was on the contrary to be rather hesitant. Topography does much to explain why; for the Lorraine gateway, though easier going than the slopes of the Vosges on the south or the Moselle plateau to the north, is by no means the open plain that a hasty glance at the map suggests. It is rolling rather than flat, much broken up in places and interspersed with patches of thick woodland. Militarily the most important features are the waterways, the Seille and Petite Seille rivers on the left, the belt of marshy lakes joined by the Sarr Canal in the centre and the River Sarr on the right. All lay generally parallel to the French line of advance. They are com-

manded by low ridges, almost everywhere covered by dense forest. Tactical prudence demanded that the French should secure the cornerstones of the Lorraine gateway before entering, by sending troops to seize the crests of the Vosges on the right and to mask the dominating Delme ridge on the left; the principles of march security laid down that they should advance on a continuous front, clearing the woodlands and the high ground between the waterways of lurking Germans. But urgency and security tend always to militate against each other, and so they did here. For though it proved easy enough to secure the 'cornerstones', it was to be found much more difficult to deploy marching columns off the roads, which followed the river valleys, and still maintain a reasonable marching speed.

Both armies began by showing caution however, and neither made more than a few miles in the first day of the offensive, 14th August. It was not until the next that either crossed the line of the frontier, which had been abandoned for diplomatic reasons a fortnight before. Neither had encountered measured resistance, for though there were Germans who stood and fought for the isolated position, most seemed content to be off as soon as the French appeared, using their plentiful artillery of all calibres to cover their retreat and harass the attackers.

Progress on 16th August was a little quicker, the advance guards of both armies reaching positions some eight miles north-east of their line of departure. Already however the terrain had begun to impose its own logic on the pattern of operations, causing the axes of the two armies to diverge and their subordinate corps to attack on separate fronts. Foch's XX Corps, on the left of Second Army, itself protected on the left by IX and XVIII Corps to the east of Nancy, found itself attracted into the valley of the Petite Seille, which leads via Moyenvic and Château Salins to Morhange;

Dubail

Castelnau

Foch

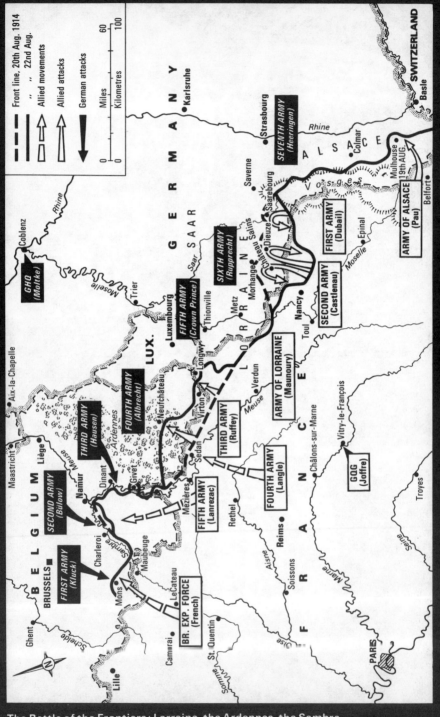

The Battle of the Frontiers: Lorraine, the Ardennes, the Sambre

XV Corps in the centre was drawn into the valley of the Seille and on towards Dieuze; while XVI Corps on the right, acting as flank guard, had difficulty in keeping up over virtually trackless territory and virtually no success in maintaining contact with First Army.

That was partly because First Army was making its way nearer east than north-eastwards and, confined to a fairly narrow corridor between the belt of lakes and the shoulders of the Vosges, was itself having trouble in protecting its flanks. The three cavalry divisions, now formed into a corps under General Conneau, the senior divisional commander, had been allotted the vital rôle of liaison between the two armies but at no stage was in close touch with either, nor, it would seem, with the enemy. The right wing of First Army, consisting of XIV and XXI Corps, were fighting battles of their own, the latter seeking to seize the peak of the Donon to the main body's right rear, the former to debouch eastward over the Vosges crests. Pau's Army of Alsace, following the same route as Bonneau had taken a week earlier, was making independently for Mulhouse.

This scattered advance across territory poorly served by lateral roads and in an age of still primitive signal communications, exposed both armies to the danger of surprise attack and defeat in detail. The danger was heightened by the failure of either commander to keep a tactical reserve under his hand and by the inability of the cavalry to scout effectively among the lakes and woods. Dubail was alert to this danger and on 16th August he ordered the main body of XXI Corps to disengage in the Vosges and march to his right, at the same time pressing Castelnau to extend towards him across the lake region. This Castelnau was unwilling to do, since his own left wing was about to be weakened by the transfer, on Joffre's direction, of XVIII Corps to the Belgian frontier.

The paths of the vanguards continued therefore to diverge and in the puzzling absence of concerted enemy resistance – all the more puzzling in view of his occasionally stubborn defence of a ridge or village and by his continuous drenching of the zone of advance with heavy calibre shellfire from battery positions beyond the range of the French seventy-fives – the temptation to cover ground rather than organise a solid front grew ever stronger. Evidence of this trend became apparent on 17th August and unmistakeable the following day when XV Corps of Second Army pushed quickly into Dieuze in the valley of the Seille and VIII Corps of First Army raced a regiment into Sarrebourg, as soon as it was discovered to be empty. On 19th August Foch's corps, which hitherto had lagged rather behind the rest of Second Army, came within sight of Morhange, the other major town on the armies' front, after an advance of over eight miles.

Such gains of ground made a heartening display on Joffre's situation map. A cautious observer however might have found cause for disquiet in the existence of salients of uncleared territory along the front of advance, particularly one to the left in the Forest of Koecking, which covers the high ground between the valleys of the Petite Seille, which was occupied by XX Corps, and the Seille, on which XV and XVI Corps were operating; and another in the centre, where the boundary between First and Second Armies bordered the Forest of Fénétrange. Both of these heavily wooded salients provided covered assembly areas for an enemy counterattack (perhaps by those 'three corps' of Seventh Army which GQG's Intelligence section had marked as 'unlocated' for the last six days). And anxieties might well have been heightened by the suddenly increased resistance which Dubail's soldiers had met throughout 19th August as they tried to press on up the Sarrebourg – Phalsbourg road. This, leading as it does to the narrow saddle of the Vosges at Saverne, is the natural exit from the

Lorraine gateway to the Rhine Valley, and a crucial objective of the Lorraine offensive.

Dubail's nerves had been attuned for warning signals of a counter-offensive throughout the last two days. Few enough had come his way but his suspicions were accurate, for the German Sixth and Seventh Armies (known to GQG only as the Armies of Lorraine and Alsace, so defective was its grasp of the German order of battle) were indeed preparing a counter-stroke. Their commanders had surrendered the ground they had only with reluctance and, from the first moments of the French advance, they had continued to petition Moltke for permission to go over to an offensive rôle.

He had consistently refused, for the good reason that his plans demanded inactivity on the German left, an inactivity which it was hoped would tempt the French into so deeply committing their armies of the right that by the time the proportions of the German invasion of Belgium had become apparent it would be too late to extricate them for transfer to the north.

Since their combined strength fell only a little short of their opponents' – Sixth Army controlling five corps (from left to right, III and II Bavarian, XXI, I Bavarian and I Bavarian Reserve) and Seventh Army three (XIV, XV and XIV Reserve) – the two commanding generals, Prince Rupprecht of Bavaria and von Heeringen, found their allotted rôle almost inexplicable. Krafft von Delmensingen, Rupprecht's Chief of Staff, found it inexcusable. Aware though he was of Schlieffen's conception of using the German left as bait with which to tempt the French right into the Lorraine gateway, he urged on Moltke's headquarters (OHL) two powerful if incompatible arguments against an extended retreat:

First, that it would open a gap between Sixth and Seventh Armies into which the French might lunge.

Second, that if allowed to advance

Heeringen

freely the French would transfer their uncommitted forces to oppose the German First and Second Armies in Belgium.

It was the second argument which proved the more convincing. On 17th August an emissary arrived from OHL at Sixth Army Headquarters with word that there were indeed signs of some French troop movement from Lorraine to Belgium. And although he forbade counterattack to fix the remainder in place, he did so on the purely tactical grounds that such an attack would have to be frontal – a method anathema to German staff teaching. Scenting indecision, Krafft and Rupprecht intensified their arguments to which, late on 18th August, the operations section at OHL effectively yielded by announcing that it would not oblige Krafft with a direct refusal, 'if he persisted in asking for operational freedom of action'. He replied that if the decision was to be left to him, he would mount a counterattack as soon as could be.

Auspiciously, a re-adjustment of force by each side had just granted him a slight numerical advantage.

Krafft von Delmensingen

Rupprecht of Bavaria

Castelnau had lost XVIII and most of IX Corps, requisitioned by Joffre to stiffen the northern end of the line, and had gained only the 2nd Group of (three) Reserve Divisions in exchange. Rupprecht and Heeringen however had recently been allotted five of the ten available *Ersatz* divisions, ad hoc units weak in artillery but formed from young reservists and so constituting a powerful increase of infantry strength. Krafft had further reinforced the Lorraine gateway by bringing two of Heeringen's three corps up from their original positions opposite the Belfort gap and inserting them on Sixth Army's left between the lake region and the shoulders of the Vosges. Dubail and Castelnau therefore deployed seven corps and three reserve divisions against eight corps and five *Ersatz* divisions. Moreover one of their corps was isolated in the Vosges (though so too was one of the German); the 2nd Group of Reserve Divisions was committed to cover Nancy rather than manoeuvre offensively where it was needed on Castelnau's left wing; and Pau's Army of Alsace, though opposed only

by *Landwehr* units, was too deeply engaged before Mulhouse to lend assistance. In the Lorraine gateway itself, therefore, the French deployed only eleven divisions to the Germans' nineteen; and their superiority in cavalry (three divisions to two) was nullified by its seeming inability to find and keep in touch with the enemy.

That the enemy was close about him, and in greater numbers than in the opening days of the campaign, Dubail did not doubt. He estimated however that a further attack, if rapid and determined, would probably suffice to chase them out of their positions and open the road to Saverne and the Rhine. On the evening of 19th August he therefore warned the commander of the 15th Division that it would have to undertake a night march of eight miles and then mount a dawn attack on the bridges of the Sarre beyond Sarrebourg, where its sister division, 16th, had been heavily engaged all day. The division arrived at its forming-up positions at four next morning, 20th August, an hour later than intended and tired after a march over unfamiliar roads, but

A battery of French 75mm field guns

The French 75mm field gun, France's equivalent to the 18-pounder, was one of the world's great guns, and the French had an almost religious faith in its capabilities, which were very good. It was easy to fire and maintain, and was extremely accurate. *Calibre:* 75mm. *Weight of shell:* 16 pounds (shrapnel). *Weight of gun and carriage:* 2,657 pounds. *Range:* 7,440 yards. *Elevation:* —10° to +19°. *Rate of fire:* six rounds per minute was normal, but in desperate situations it was not unknown for crews to fire at the rate of twenty rounds per minute

A French 75mm field gun and ammunition limber

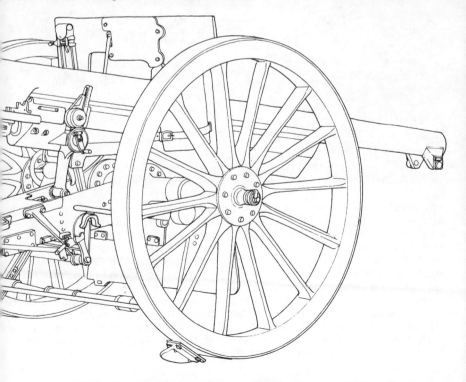

nevertheless moved briskly into the attack. Its first objective was carried at bayonet point and the columns pressed on northwards nearly a mile up the Sarre valley. Then an overwhelming barrage fire descended on the leading waves and from the woods on each side burst continuous volleys of rifle and machine-gun fire. The Battle of Sarrebourg had begun.

The 15th Division was quickly driven out of its advanced positions and retired to the high ground west of the town, thereby escaping the worst of the unrelenting bombardment. At mid-morning it swelled in intensity and the German infantry, hitherto concealed in the surrounding forests, suddenly appeared in solid masses marching straight on Sarrebourg itself. The town was held by the 16th Division, which had already suffered heavily the day before. Against the furious assault of I

German infantry advancing to attack in Lorraine

Bavarian Corps, it nevertheless held firm, giving ground only very slowly on the outskirts of the town and then contesting it street by street under growing pressure. The 95th Regiment, in the centre of the town itself, threw up barricades of barrels and furniture, loopholed the houses and made a redoubt of the German cavalry barracks which commanded the main street. Throughout the afternoon it fought as stoutly as

French infantry knew how. By four in the afternoon, after over a thousand men, a third of the regiment's strength, had been killed or disabled, and with no sign of reinforcement marching to their support, it had become clear that the survivors could hold Sarrebourg no longer. Their divisional – soon to be army – Com-

Maud'huy

mander, de Maud'huy, issued the order to disengage and stood to review the regiment as it passed southwards out of the town, calling on the band to strike up the Marche Lorraine as a parting gesture. Then he took up his place with the rearguard, '*son éternelle pipe à la bouche*'.

The loss of Sarrebourg, though disheartening, did not spell defeat to Dubail; his other two corps, though also assailed all day by XIV and XV Corps, had given little ground and was still in fighting trim. If his left flank, resting on the lake region, was still covered by Second Army, he saw no reason why he should not accept the day's events as a local reverse and, after regrouping, resume the offensive. Of Second Army however he had had no word since morning. When news came, it was of outright disaster, disposing for good of any notion of further advance, indeed threatening the whole right wing, from Pont à Mousson to Belfort, with defeat in the open field.

It had dawned misty on Second Army's front, as so often that hot August, and Castelnau accordingly decided to postpone moving off until visibility improved. The troops had breakfasted and broken camp and were formed up in their overnight positions which they had not entrenched. On those positions, at about five in the morning, a violent bombardment suddenly descended and a few minutes later, wave upon wave, followed the infantry of XXI and I Bavarian Reserve Corps. They concentrated undetected in the forests of Fénétrange and Koecking whence, pouring down in converging columns, they quickly carried all before them. The soldiers of XV and XVI Corps, southerners from Marseilles and Toulon, were seized by a sudden and infectious panic, abandoned their positions and poured rearward, carrying with them all but a few battalions of Chasseurs. Within a few hours the fleetest fugitives had crossed the line from which they had set out a week earlier. Dubail's left flank was exposed along its whole length. Foch's XX Corps at Morhange was threatened with encirclement, as the Reserve Divisions on his left also gave way before the attack of the III Bavarian Corps, and if he abandoned his position, Nancy itself would be lost.

But Foch's men were natives of the region, less volatile than the southerners – so the post-mortems went – and were supported on their left by one of those splendid brigades of white Colonials who time and again in the Battle of the Frontiers were to demonstrate how superior regular troops were to conscript – however brave – in a crisis. Hustled out of its overnight positions, XX Corps nevertheless kept its ranks steady and under Foch's firm control established a new line around Château Salins from which it repelled every attack the Bavarians launched against it. So successful indeed was its defence that at the very moment when the order to retreat arrived, the troops had the impression that victory was at hand. The order was inevitable, however, given the total disruption of de Castelnau's front and under cover of darkness XX Corps set off to rejoin the rest of Second and First Armies in a forced march to the line of the Meurthe. By morning it had left the Bavarians twelve miles behind.

Castelnau's initial assessment of the result of the Battle of Morhange was that it would mean abandoning Nancy and falling back as far as the Moselle. This Joffre categorically forbade. Fortunately the Sixth and Seventh Armies did not press their pursuit and it was not until 25th August that their advance guards appeared on the river Meurthe. In the three days which had intervened the French had recovered themselves remarkably, organised a powerful front, particularly on the mountain known as the Grand Couronné east of Nancy, and were ready to resist whatever onslaughts the Germans might make on it. Those were to be heavy, for their success in Lorraine had kindled in OHL's thinking the notion of a double envelopment of the French armies, which was not to be extinguished until the Battle of the Marne had settled the issue in the west for good.

Why had Joffre's first offensive failed so lamentably? The conventional explanation is that the French cast themselves to destruction in a frenzy of offensive ardour. A more careful examination of the conduct of the Lorraine campaign suggests that it was rather due to a neglect of elementary military principles. Neither Dubail nor Castelnau had maintained a proper tactical reserve, reconnoitred their axes of advance or organised continuous fronts. As a result their lines had been easily infiltrated and their infantry ambushed in undefended positions. These were not conclusions, however, which Joffre yet seemed ready to draw. On 22nd August he was to start Third and Fourth Armies on an ominously similar offensive into the even more broken and densely forested territory of the Ardennes.

Third Army, commanded by Ruffey with his headquarters at Verdun, and

Ruffey

Fourth, commanded by de Langle de Cary with his headquarters at St Dizier, amounted to a very considerable force: three cavalry divisions, twenty first-line infantry divisions, of which three were Active Colonial and two Reserve divisions, in all some 360,000 men. Their mission, as laid down in Plan XVII and confirmed by Joffre in his orders of 20th August, was simple and straightforward: to push into the Ardennes, which he conceived to be unoccupied, with the eventual object of joining First and Second Armies' attack on the German centre at Metz-Thionville. To hold the gap between these two major concentrations, Joffre had created on 21st August the Army of Lorraine, composed entirely of reserve divisions, based at Verdun under the command of General Maunoury. Its task would be to hold the line of the Meuse around the fortress should the German centre advance westward.

Since the German centre was not located at Metz, since indeed the German army had no 'centre' in any conventional sense, the Army of Lorraine was not to be put to the test.

A French outpost line in the Argonne

De Langle de Cary

Albrecht von Württemberg

The German Crown Prince

Maunoury

The Third and Fourth Armies, however, were about to undergo a very severe ordeal indeed for as they began their advance north-eastward into the Ardennes, expecting to meet nothing more troublesome than a thin cavalry screen, two large German armies began their march south-westward on a collision course. These, the Fourth under the Duke of Württemberg, and the Fifth, under the German Crown Prince, were probably the superior, certainly the equal of the French in strength: twenty divisions, six *Landwehr* brigades and two cavalry divisions, in all about 380,000 men.

The original mission of this very large German concentration had been to act as the pivot of the 'great wheel' and it was not intended that it should make any concerted or extended move against the French until the right wing had made a good deal more headway into northern France than it had by 21st August. The news of Rupprecht's success over Dubail and Castelnau which came that day to Knöbelsdorff, the Crown Prince's Chief of Staff (and de facto commander of his army) stirred him to beg OHL for permission to undertake a similar advance and, with certain reservations, it was granted. Hence the certainty of collision the following day.

Collision – a head-on blundering into each other – it turned out to be. The Ardennes is an area almost impossible to reconnoitre effectively – a fact from which Hitler's panzer columns were to profit greatly in two memorable campaigns of the Second World War. The terrain is very broken, densely wooded, sparsely traversed by roads and much cut up by streams and small but fast-flowing rivers which run across the line of east-west movement.

The Germans had, nevertheless, made some effort to explore the forest and for some days their IV Cavalry Corps had been operating within it. They had not been able to discover the whereabouts of the French, for the very good reason that neither Dubail's nor de Langle's army had yet entered it, but had familiarised themselves to some extent with the terrain and the difficulties of operating across it. The French enjoyed no such advantage, indeed few of their units had been supplied with adequate maps, many battalion officers being forced to work from sheets torn from railway timetables.

The formation adopted by the French, who were aligned generally north-west/south-east with Fourth Army on the left and Third on the right, has been likened to a flight of steps, each step being formed by a corps which, because of its staggered position in the line of battle, might face to fight the enemy either northwards or eastwards. In fact, as is always the case with a staggered or echeloned deployment, the failure of any one corps to make progress would mean that its neighbour to the left would have to halt also, for fear of exposing itself to attack in flank and rear. This danger could, of course, be overcome if neighbouring units were able to come quickly enough to each others' assistance but, as in the Lorraine gateway, the nature of the terrain and the absence of effective communications was to make liaison almost impossible. Conditions, indeed, were to ensure that the action was to be of the most confused and uncoordinated kind.

The battles which broke out on the morning of 22nd August are known to the French as those of Virton and the Semois, to the Germans as those of Longwy and Neufchâteau, but although these three places and that river indeed saw much of the fighting, it was too inchoate and unlocalised to bear such precise nomenclature. Their nature can best be grasped in terms of the 'flight of steps' analogy.

First of the French to meet opposition was the centre corps of Ruffey's Third Army, which bumped into the XIII Corps soon after dawn as the

Above: German infantry on the frontier
Below: German infantry waiting to go forward

Above: A German patrol in the Argonne
Below: Hastily dug German entrenchments in the Argonne

French infantry on the line of march

Germans were preparing to attack. Caught unawares and off balance, V Corps collapsed and broke for the rear, and its neighbours, Sarrail's VI and Boëlle's IV Corps, though putting up much stouter resistance, were compelled by the afternoon to retreat and to halt respectively.

Boëlle's failure to make progress meant that the commander of the corps to his left, which formed the right flank of de Langle's Fourth Army, realised that his flank would become exposed if he advanced and flinched therefore from doing so. On *his left*, the Colonial Corps, flower of de Langle's, and arguably of the whole French army, was in no wise deterred from pressing forward. It would have surprised all if it had been, for its three divisions were composed of regulars who had served their time in North Africa, Madagascar and Indo-China, men equal in experience to the contemptibles of the BEF and as bold and skilful in battle (though unfortunately trained in the heretical school of the bayonet instead of the bullet). Directed to seize the town of Neufchâteau and its environs, the colonials advanced with a will, brushing aside the skirmishers who attempted to block their passage along the narrow, thicket-lined roads and ignoring the Uhlans, who sniped at them with their carbines from the undergrowth.

The vanguard of the corps was deployed in two columns, to the left the 5th Colonial Brigade, to the right and separated from it by a tract of peculiarly dense Ardennes woodland, the leading brigade of the 3rd Colonial Division. Both expected to join hands

at Neufchâteau, on which their separate routes converged. Both were halted by resolute German opposition well short of their objective. The 5th Brigade, though furiously assailed, stood its ground and inflicted terrible losses on the doughty but inexperienced German reservists who barred its way. The leading brigade of the 3rd Colonial Division, attempting to force a passage forward, were checked and suffered a horrifying fate. This episode, in fact, has perhaps contributed most to the legend of the 'martyrdom of the French infantry' in the Marne campaign.

Five French battalions were engaged in all, deployed because of the terrain one behind the other on a front only 600 yards wide. Their opponents comprised nine battalions, a dismounted cavalry regiment and a battalion of sappers, 'methodically deployed on a wide front that extended far beyond both French flanks'. Into this trap the Colonials launched one bayonet charge after another, trying to beat down a hail of artillery, machine gun and rifle fire with bare steel. It was a bloodily unsuccessful attempt, and eventually the brigade was compelled to fall back into the village of Rossignol, having lost most of its officers – three of the five battalion commanders were killed by a single burst of machine-gun fire while conferring at the roadside.

Rossignol lay however on the wrong side of the Semois, passage across which the Germans were able to bait by playing an impenetrable curtain of shrapnel on the only bridge. The brigade was thus unable to retreat: its sister brigade was unable to come to its aid, and was in any case itself under heavy pressure because of the failure of a neighbouring formation to protect its flank. By nightfall the 3rd Colonial Division, having lost 11,000 of its 17,000 men killed, wounded or missing, including its commander and one of its brigade commanders dead, the other brigade commander wounded and taken prisoner and most of its artillery captured, could no longer be counted in the French order of battle.

The defeat of the Colonial Corps meant the defeat of de Langle's Fourth Army and that, in turn, entailed the failure of the Ardennes offensive. Joffre enjoined a continuation of effort the following day but no part of either army could make headway and on the night of 24th August Joffre approved the retirement of Fourth Army across the Meuse. Ruffey and Manoury were to persist a little longer though without hope of success. But by the evening of 23rd August, Joffre's attention and anxieties (if he had any, for he displayed none) had been turned to the extreme left of his front, where Lanrezac's Fifth Army and the British Expeditionary Force had taken up station on the river Sambre.

Liège and the Sambre

The success of Germany's War Plan supposed two preconditions: the seizing of the Belgian and Luxembourgois railways networks and the destruction of the Belgian forts on the Meuse. Luxembourg was in no position to offer resistance to a German invasion and was occupied without opposition on the morning of 2nd August.

Belgium presented more of an obstacle. It possessed an army. Admittedly its army had defects – a lack of officers, of modern equipment, of experience, above all of trained reserves – but it could field a force to stand in Germany's way if its king and his cabinet so decided. The Kaiser sought to deter them by a clear warning of his intention to

Belgian Militia in a roadblock, August 1914

march across their country whatever their wishes, but King Albert and his government refused to be cowed. The Belgian army had already mobilised and they ordered it to concentrate along the River Gette, a tributary of the Scheldt which forms a defensive line covering Brussels from the east. Albert's own strategy was for the army to deploy along the line of the Meuse, filling the gaps in the fortified line from Liège to Namur, but the council of war which met to decide Belgian plans on 2nd August persuaded him against allotting any more than two divisions to this 'forward' strategy. That left four infantry divisions, plus a cavalry division, to defend the capital.

The security of Belgium depended, however, not upon her field army, certainly not upon her citizen militia, bravely though it was to assist the regulars in the coming weeks, but upon her great fortresses. Antwerp, the largest, was out of the direct line of invasion. Liège and Namur stood immediately in the Germans' path. Indeed, until they had been reduced, neither First nor Second Armies could reach the positions from which they were to launch their decisive strokes against the French left. The Great General Staff had accordingly earmarked a special task force of thirteen Active infantry regiments, which were to be withdrawn from their

German artillerymen bringing a 210mm howitzer into action

King Albert

Emmich

parent divisions at the outbreak, and committed immediately to the seizure of the outermost of the two vital *place-forts*, Liège. The force was to be commanded by a man of energy and decision, von Emmich, and provided with siege batteries of the heaviest calibres, 210mm mortars, later to be supplemented by Skoda and Krupp howitzers of even greater power.

The Belgians were as resolved to defend Liège as the Germans to take it. Leman, the newly appointed commander, received an order, in the king's own hand, which charged him 'to hold to the end with your division the position which you have been entrusted to defend' and this the general was determined to do. His main deficiency was in infantry. Liège, like Namur, was a 'ring' fortress, of twelve isolated forts grouped round a central citadel. Tactical theory demanded that the gaps in the ring be entrenched and filled with 'interval troops', but he had been given neither the time nor the men to do either.

Unfortunately for the German task force, their commanders had counted

on Liège being almost ungarrisoned (they expected to find there only 6,000 instead of the 35,000 men Leman disposed of) and of their being able therefore to infiltrate the defences undetected, or at least unopposed, under cover of darkness. On the night of 5th-6th August, the assault troops were formed up into five columns and started off on converging paths towards the centre of Liège. All were quickly checked by fire, either from the forts or from the newly-joined infantry of 3rd Division. Recognising that the plan was on the brink of failure its author, Ludendorff placed himself at the head of one of the halted columns and ordered it forward. After a bitter fight, he broke into the centre of the fortified area and found himself overlooking the city of Liège and its undamaged bridges. He had lost contact with the Germans outside the perimeter however and decided not to press his advantage until he had been reinforced. After a wait of twenty-four hours he had still not re-established touch and therefore determined to take the risk of plunging straight on for the centre of the fortress. Arriving

Leman

Ludendorff

unchallenged outside the citadel, where he expected to meet a reconnaissance party he had sent on ahead, and finding no one about, he surmised that they had got into the citadel, banged on the door with his sword pommel and was as surprised as the occupants when it was opened by Belgian soldiers. Fortunately they proved ready to surrender. By noon on 7th August, therefore, Ludendorff had made himself master of the city of Liège.

But this did not bring free passage of the Meuse any closer within German grasp, for the outlying forts, in which the real strength of the fortress lay, were still spiritedly resisting the German assault. *Coup de main* having recognisably failed, the German high command accordingly decided upon deliberate siege, the initial resort to which they had rejected on the grounds that it would impose more delay on operations than their timetable would stand.

Deliberate siege was indeed a time-consuming business, but the Germans were better equipped to bring a siege to an expeditious close than any

other army in Europe. Foreseeing the possibility of static warfare, which the French had refused on doctrinal grounds to envisage or make provision for, they had designed and built the biggest mobile artillery pieces in the world: 420mm Krupp siege howitzers. They had also borrowed from the Austrians a number of the next biggest pieces, 305mm Skoda howitzers. These were ordered up on 8th August. Two 420mm howitzers left the Krupp works on 10th August and were emplaced on the 12th. Firing began immediately. It was an awe-inspiring performance. A minute passed between discharge and arrival, the shell reaching a height of 12,000 feet before plunging down to penetrate the forts' concrete or armour-plate skin at almost right-angle impact – the secret of its penetrative power. Waiting for the shots to fall stretched the nerves of the Belgian garrisons to breaking point; worst of all was the sound of the explosions being 'walked' inexorably across the surrounding terrain and up to the concrete heart of the defences. Few of the forts could hold out, either physically or psy-

One of the 305mm Austrian Skoda
Siege Howitzers which destroyed the
Belgian fortresses

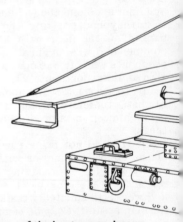

The Austro-Hungarian Skoda 305mm howitzer was one of the best super-heavy
guns of the war, as was proved initially on the Western Front against Maubeuge
and Liége, and continually on the Eastern Front, where it was used in greater
numbers, against fortresses such as Przemysl and against such defensive
strongpoints that the Russians managed to build. It was surprisingly mobile,
considering its enormous weight, as it could be broken down into easily moveable
sections for transport. Emplaced, it weighed about 28 tons, and normally had a
crew of twelve to fire it, but this was variable, depending on the circumstances,
particularly the rate of fire desired. Its maximum range was 13,124 yards firing the
standard weight shell of 846 pounds, and a normal rate of fire was about ten rounds
per hour. The destructive capabilities of this gun were enormous, especially as no

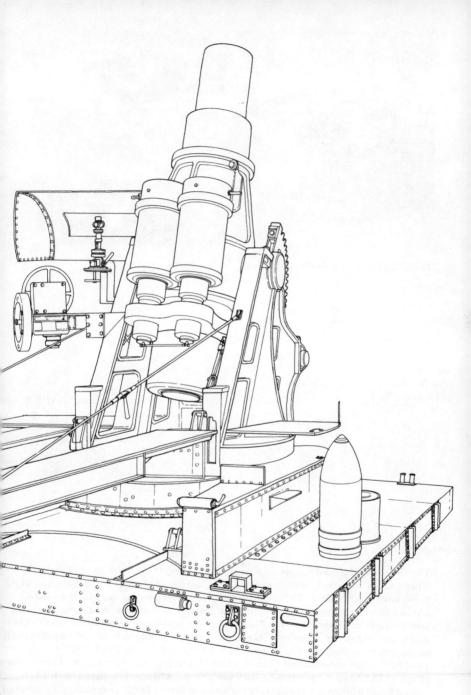

orts in use during the opening stages of the First World War had been designed to
:ake plunging fire from guns of so large a calibre. The 305mm howitzer had been
designed (at Pilsen in 1910) to be road transportable and to be reassembled quickly –
:he latter took a mere 40 minutes.

The effect of siege artillery at Liége

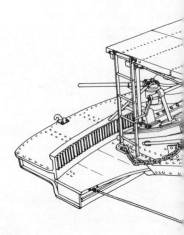

The Germans also had a huge howitzer, one far larger than the Skoda in fact – the Krupp 42cm howitzer, known as the *'Dicke Bertha'*. This was the largest gun of its time, and like the Skoda 30.5cm howitzer, its pulverising high angle fire was completely irresistable. If the mobility of the Skoda howitzer was remarkable, so was that of the Krupp monster. This was designed to be moved by rail, and to that end could be broken down into five major sub-parts. Reassembly of the parts took six hours, considerably longer than the time needed for the Skoda 305. Emplaced, the 42cm howitzer weighed 75 tons, could fire ten rounds per hour, had a maximum range of 15,530 yards and fired a shell weighing 2,520 pounds, fitted with a delayed action fuse to allow it to penetrate far into the target before exploding. Illustrated is one of the two special 42cm howitzers adapted just before the war to be road transportable, when the Germans realised that the expected speed of their initial advance would be slowed if their super-heavy guns could not keep up with them. A battery of two of these weapons required a crew of 280 men.

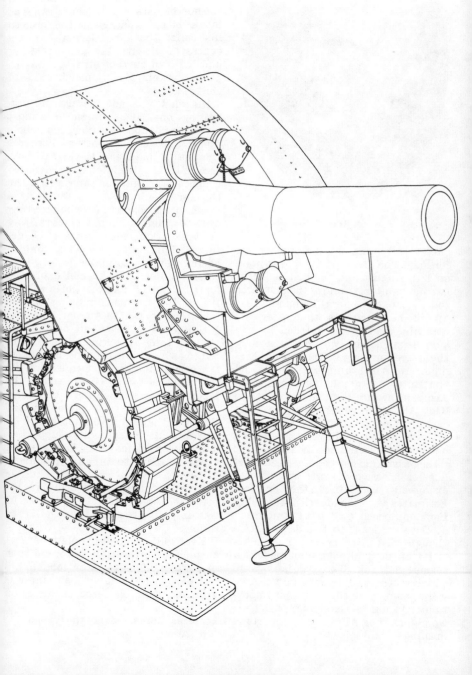

Bülow

chologically, against such treatment for long. The first surrendered at noon on 13th August and the last seventy-two hours later. In one of the last forts to be attacked General Leman had set up his headquarters and, after the magazine had been exploded by the bombardment, he was found among the dazed survivors. His captor, Emmich, returned him his sword and von Bülow, commanding the Second Army, allowed him to send a letter to King Albert, in which he wrote 'I am certain of having sustained the honour of our arms. I have surrendered neither the fortress nor the forts'.

Liège had indeed been a gallant (if hopeless) passage of arms, with results extremely frustrating to the Germans. Estimates as to the length of the delay Leman imposed vary, but it amounted at the very least to two days. Little though that may seem, the inelasticity of the Schlieffen plan made it a serious setback. The Belgian army, which was shortly to retire upon Antwerp and play no rôle of major importance again in the campaign, had thus won for the Allies an important opening advantage.

The advantage would have been greater had it been recognised. Joffre, however, to whom the *coup de main* of 6th August might have sounded a warning, remained resolutely unmoved by any suspicion of danger to the north-eastern frontier of France as late as 14th August. He still adhered to his belief that the German army's centre of gravity lay around Metz; and his own current strategy was to attack pre-emptively on either side of that place.

His view was not merely the prevailing one. It commanded almost unaminous support among his subordinates. The only important dissenter was the commander of the Fifth Army, Lanrezac. He, like Michel, the deposed Chief of Staff, did not believe that the Germans could resist so tempting a means of approach to French territory as that which Belgium and its railway network provided. Moreover he detected signs which seemed to confirm their intention to make use of it. As early as 31st July he had expressed fears for his left flank in the eventuality of the Germans moving to the lower Meuse. On 5th August, when his Intelligence section had established that the force attacking Liège amounted to as many as six corps, he requested permission at least to extend his left wing as far as Givet, where the Meuse enters Belgian territory. Thanks in part to a threat by the Belgians that they would fall back on Antwerp if not speedily supported, Joffre granted leave for Lanrezac's I Corps to move to Dinant, just north of Givet; but since he wished to use the rest of Lanrezac's army in his projected attack into the Ardennes, he was unwilling to allow the rest of it to follow.

Meanwhile he kept his plans dark. A suspicion, however, of the trend both of Joffre's offensive intentions and of German operations in Belgium was growing upon Lanrezac, a suspicion

Lanrezac, Commander of the French Fifth Army

German infantry goosestepping
through Brussels

German
infantry in Brussels

Succour for the enemy. A Belgian
priest turns the other cheek

Franchet d'Esperey

which, if accurate, he recognised as holding the gravest consequences not only for his own army, most exposed of the five though it was, but for the whole of the French array. It was a suspicion, however, to which it was difficult to give substance, since GQG's Intelligence section consistently minimised the number of German corps in Belgium in its estimates, ignored its prewar judgement that the enemy would employ reserve corps in the first-line, treated all Belgian Intelligence as rumour and accepted the failure of Sordet's cavalry corps to make contact with the Germans between Liège and the Ardennes as evidence of their absence.

By 14th August Lanrezac made up his mind to face Joffre in person. It was an amiable but unfruitful interview which ensued. Lanrezac's manner has been described as professorial and Joffre did not like to be lectured. He dismissed all Lanrezac's arguments against continuing with preparations for the offensive into the Ardennes and, as to the danger from beyond the Sambre and Meuse, he felt, he said, that 'the Germans have nothing ready

there'. Lanrezac pointed out to Joffre's assistants when the interview was over that their own Intelligence estimates put the German strength in Belgium at six corps which, since it equalled that of his own army and the British Expeditionary Force – now marching towards Maubeuge – combined, was a factor which no plan for an offensive into the Ardennes could leave out of account. But they too proffered him only reassurances.

On his return to Fifth Army headquarters, however, Lanrezac found awaiting him a new GQG Intelligence estimate which acknowledged the presence of eight German corps in Belgium – evidence that light had at last begun to penetrate General Headquarters, if not to the Chief's sanctum. The events of the following day, 15th August brought news which even Joffre could not ignore: news that the Germans had seized the bridges of the Meuse at Huy, midway between Namur and Liège, and that Franchet d'Esperey's I Corps had been assailed at Dinant, suffering a thousand casualties before driving the Germans off.

Joffre did not ignore the news. At 3.30pm he issued an amendment to his plan of campaign which for the first time acknowledged that the Sambre and Meuse line was menaced by the enemy. His Special Directive No 10 ordered Lanrezac to transfer his army from its concentration area northwards into the angle formed by the confluence of the two rivers at Namur. He was to leave behind his XI Corps, which would join Fourth Army for the Ardennes operation, but to receive in exchange XVIII Corps, at that moment entraining in Lorraine. The 2nd Group of (three) Reserve Divisions at Vervins, and Sordet's Cavalry Corps, still vainly beating empty countryside across the Meuse, were also to come under his command. As two of his three original corps (III and X – though not I) had recently received a third division (those mobilised from the French population of Algeria) Joffre's redisposition gave

German railway troops leaving to work on the damaged Belgian railways

him a substantially strengthened command - ten Active, three Reserve and three cavalry divisions - to undertake his independent mission.

Joffre also stipulated, however, that he must for the moment regard his mission as a precautionary one: 'to act in concert with the British army and Belgian forces against the opposing forces in the north'. Joffre offered no estimate of how strong those forces might be. Not until 18th August did he reveal his mind more clearly when, in Special Directive No 13, issued to Fifth, Fourth and Third Armies, he described two strategic possibilities and outlined the measures to be taken. Whichever materialised, his supposition was that German strength in Belgium had increased from less than six to between thirteen and fifteen corps, of which eight seemed to be advancing north of the Sambre and Meuse, the rest through the Ardennes. The latter in any case were to be engaged by Fourth and Third Armies, whose departure

was imminent, and it was possible that those armies would find that a portion of the German force presently above the Sambre and Meuse would by then have joined those in the Ardennes, leaving only a fraction in northern Belgium. If the Germans corps north of the Sambre joined those below it, the Fifth Army was to leave the Sambre lines to be guarded by the Belgians or the BEF, and itself turn east to support Fourth Army's drive into the Ardennes. His second hypothesis was that the eight German corps of the northern group might 'seek to pass between Givet and Brussels and even to accentuate its movement further to the north': in which case the BEF, the Belgians and the Fifth Army should march to outflank the Germans from the west.

The situation still remained unclear when the advance guards of III and X Corps reached the banks of the

Sambre between Charleroi and Namur on the afternoon of 20th August. They had marched sixty miles during the previous five days. Spears, the British liaison officer at Lanrezac's headquarters, who had passed and repassed their long columns on his missions during those days, records that 'The men were cheerful and gay, in spite of the fatigues imposed on them by the constant marching in torrid weather. The reservists were obviously getting fit, and indeed, under the gruelling they were being submitted to, it was a question of getting fit or dying of exhaustion'.

But their commander was far from cheerful. He feared for his left flank, which would remain quite without support until and unless the BEF came up. He feared also for the security of his right, which was menaced by the enemy's advance into the Ardennes (not yet checked by the Fourth Army's offensive). He was deeply frustrated by Joffre's seeming indifference to the peril which threatened on the Sambre; and, having reached the river, he was seized by indecision over how best to hold it.

The Meuse between Namur and Givet, which Franchet d'Esperey's I Corps was defending, forms an excellent obstacle, for it flows through a deep, sometimes precipitous trench with open country on both banks, easy to manoeuvre across and to keep under observation. But the Sambre between Namur and Charleroi is much less readily defensible. It flows through a thickly populated section – a succession of small industrial towns of factories and cottages which are tightly packed along both banks of the river, intersected by narrow cobbled streets. This region, known as the Borinage, imposes obvious tactical difficulties. Though easily to be held by small groups of infantry and machine gunners, its densely packed buildings would nullify the effects of light artillery (the principal French supporting arm), and also prevent the manoeuvre of larger

Kluck

units. In short, it was not a battlefield on which a general could expect to achieve decisive results. Lanrezac recognised that; yet he intended to force a decision nonetheless. But to add confusion, he seemed unable to choose between the only two methods of defending the river: the first, to cross the river and fight with it at his back, the second, to let the Germans cross and fight them in the open country on his side. Finally, he said nothing to his subordinates of the way his mind was working. Throughout 20th August, the commanders of III and IX Corps were left without word from him and had to make their own decisions on how best to deploy their soldiers.

Lanrezac must have guessed at the confusion his silence was causing, just as he must have realised that his subordinates' decisions might commit him irretrievably to a course of action bearing no relation to the circumstances of the British on his left or the Belgians on his right, with whom he should have been formulating a common plan. Nevertheless, he persisted in his silence, breaking it only to telegraph Joffre on the morning of 21st August to ask for advice. That was unwise. Having tried to teach the Commander-in-Chief a lesson in strategy, he was unlikely to get very sympathetic tactical guidance from him in return. Nor did he. At eight that evening, Joffre, who had just sent him instructions to open the attack, replied 'I leave it entirely to you, to judge the opportune moment for starting your offensive movement'. By then Lanrezac had finally made up his mind. That afternoon he had told his corps commanders in conference that he wished them to hold the high ground south of the river. It was too late. As his orders went out, reports of heavy fighting in the Borinage started to come in. The enemy had crossed the river and the battle, known as that of Charleroi to the French, Namur to the Germans and the Sambre to the British, had begun.

On the German side it had been preceded by a debate between the commanders of the forces advancing to the Sambre and Meuse as significant as that between Joffre and Lanrezac. Those forces were véry much larger than anyone at GQG or indeed at Lanrezac's headquarters had guessed, amounting in all to eleven infantry and two cavalry corps divided between Kluck's First Army (from east to west II, IV, IV Reserve, III, IX and II Cavalry Corps) and Bülow's Second Army (from east to west VII, VII Reserve, X Reserve, X, Guard, Guard Reserve XI and I Cavalry Corps), to which First Army had been temporarily subordinated. On 20th August, Bülow had received orders from Moltke to lay siege immediately to Namur and engage any French and Belgian forces he found on the Sambre. Meanwhile, Hausen's Third Army (from north to south, XII Reserve, XII and XIX Corps) was to thrust through the Ardennes to the Meuse between Namur and Givet and assault across it into the French flank. Details of how

Hausen

the operations were to be carried out was left entirely to the army commanders, as was normal German staff practice. OHL also supplied an Intelligence estimate, which suggested that French strength was between seven and eight corps and that the BEF had not yet reached the battle area.

Since the handling of operations on the Sambre was to be in Bülow's hands, he decided to curtail Kluck's great flank march and bring that army down directly southwards onto his own right between Charleroi and Maubeuge, the French fortress on the upper Sambre. Both Kluck and Kuhl, his Chief of Staff, disputed Bülow's decision at length and with vigour, but Bülow refused to yield. He was concerned by the apparent strength of the French concentration on the Sambre. But in forcing to conform to his own axis of advance, Bülow, though he did not know it and perhaps could not have guessed, extinguished the remaining chance of a true strategic envelopment of the Allied armies, and ensured that Kluck would run headlong into the BEF at Mons.

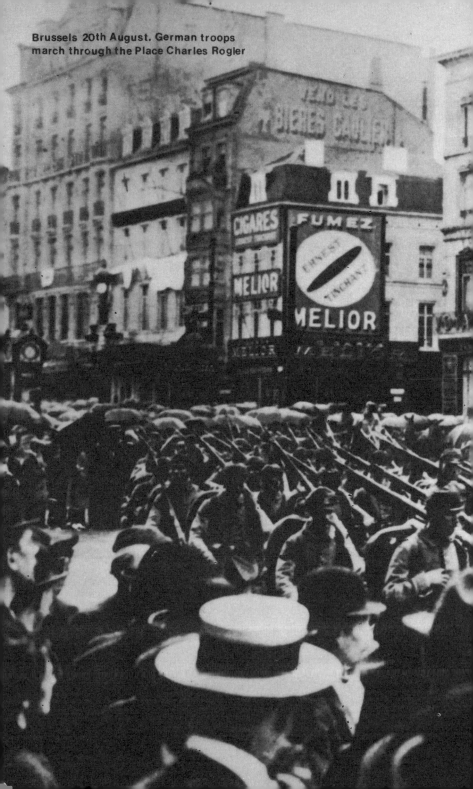

Brussels 20th August. German troops
march through the Place Charles Rogier

But Mons, though in every sense an integral and indeed crucial part of the Battle of the Frontiers, was to be a quite separate affair from that which began to unfold on the two fronts, Charleroi to Namur, and Namur to Givet, on the afternoon of 21st August. Namur itself, garrisoned by fortress troops and the 4th Belgian (Mobile) Division, was swiftly invested by two corps (Guard Reserve and XI) specially detached from Bülow's army, supported by the train of super-heavy artillery which had broken open the forts at Liège a week before. Lanrezac could send little to their aid, for he possessed no gun powerful enough to answer the giant howitzers and could spare only a brigade of infantry. Namur's fate therefore hung on the success or failure of Fifth Army's fight on the Sambre.

That fight broke out in a haphazard fashion in the afternoon of 21st August when the vanguard of X and Guard Corps, in passing south between Charleroi and Namur, encountered the French covering parties at the crossings over the Sambre between Mornimont and Roselies. Neither side was clear about what to do next. The Germans had orders not to attack that day for Bulow wished to coordinate his attack with Hausen, whom he knew would not arrive on the Namur-Givet reach of the Meuse until the next morning. The French pickets, belonging to X Corps, had an even dimmer notion of their army commander's intentions, for Lanrezac, as we have seen, had not yet made it known on which side of the river he intended to give battle. The local commanders had guessed, however that it was to be the far bank and had privately decided to hold on to the bridges from the outset rather than perhaps have to recapture them later. But their men were few in number, and after a brief reconnaissance the commander of the German 2nd Guard Division decided that he should be able to carry the bridges at Auvelais

quickly and cheaply. His corps commander, who had only shortly before received Bülow's instructions not to advance, would have forbidden the attempt had not Ludendorff, who was paying him a casual visit, overheard the discussion between them. Announcing that he would accept the responsibility himself, as he had done at Liège a fortnight before with such dramatic results, the Quartermaster-General ordered the Guard to rush the bridges.

The terrain favoured their attempt, for behind them rose the heights of La Sarte, from which their field artillery could dominate the crossing places. Of these there were eight, but only seven were defended, since the French advance guards had overlooked a railway viaduct, which they believed to be in III Corps area, when taking up their positions the night before. The Germans quickly stumbled on it, pressed across and, followed by more of the division, mounted a flank attack which drove the French

A German 77mm field battery crossing the Meuse by pontoon bridge

briskly out of Auvelais and into the village of Arsimont two miles beyond. This penetration of their line forced the rest of the X Corps pickets, which until then had been holding their positions successfully, to abandon the far bank and fall back across the river.

On III Corps' front, a similar pattern of events repeated itself. One of its detachments had also failed to protect a bridge, which the German X Corps soon discovered unguarded, and tramped across. It then set up strong positions on the south bank. Six miles of the Sambre, more if it is measured along its loops, had thus fallen to the enemy, most of it by tactical oversight. But since the fighting had been small in scale, and his losses consequently light, Lanrezac had no reason to regard the situation as hopeless it having of course never been his intention to make his principal stand in the region of the Borinage at all. Unfortunately neither his soldiers nor his officers were to know that they had not suffered a serious reverse, for

throughout the night of 21st August he quite forgot to tell anyone what his assessment of the situation was (thus mimicking the behaviour of Joffre which he himself had found so frustrating). The conclusion which his subordinates drew from the day's events was that they had suffered a defeat and, deciding that it must be reversed, the commanders of III and X Corps announced their intention to counterattack next day, 22nd August. Since by morning they had not received Lanrezac's countermand, they surmised his approval and launched their men through the morning mist into close and bloody conflict with the Prussians.

What ensued is the sort of engagement usually known as a soldiers' battle: one in which the two sides, having blundered unawares into each other, fight it out undirected by higher command until one or the other

Above: Part of Emmich's siege batteries. A 210mm mortar crew clean their gun
Below: A 210mm, cleaned and ready to fire
Right: A 210mm, in action in the heat and dust of the August advance

breaks. Thus things went that morning. It proved for the French a particularly desperate affair, for so little was the higher command aware of what was happening that the attacking infantry of X Corps were left quite without artillery support and were cut down in hundreds by the riflemen of the Prussian Guard, firing from behind cover. They also were fighting unsupervised, being ordered to quit the village of Mettet at the very moment that they had driven the French from it. Later the order was countermanded but for several hours that vital spot lay unoccupied between the two front lines. On III Corps front, the French met a full-scale counterattack (organised despite Bülow's strict forbiddance by the X Corps commander) which, like the battle around Arsimont, first blunted and then routed the French onset. By evening the whole French line had been driven back over five miles from the Sambre, and that by a force half their strength (three divisions to six). Only around Thuin, on the extreme left where their flank should have touched the BEF's (though it did not), had the French kept a foothold on the river. That was due to the arrival of XVIII Corps, a welcome reinforcement which was to be cancelled out in the balance of strength by the subsequent appearance of the German X Reserve Corps west of Charleroi, and of advance guards of VIII Corps, driving ahead of them Sordet's exhausted cavalry.

Lanrezac's report of the day's events to Joffre is remarkable on two counts: first, he wilfully and slanderously misrepresented the whereabouts of the BEF, locating it to his left rear when it was in fact already holding the line of the Condé Canal to his left front; second, he communicated his intention of moving I Corps to the support of the much battered X Corps, and of replacing it on the Meuse with

The 83rd Infantry Regiment in Namur

the 51st Reserve Division. Thus, at the moment of gravest danger to his eastern flank, he decided to relax his guard upon it, leaving a single second-line formation to withstand the advance of the whole of Hausen's Third Army.

Next morning, 23rd August, opened however less eventfully than the French had expected, the Germans being themselves in need of a pause to re-group their units before resuming the attack. When they did so, towards mid-morning, their assault again unhinged the defence, causing both XVIII and III Corps to give ground, in places as much as three miles. But on the other wing, the fighting swung markedly in the French favour, since the Guard and X Corps, apparently unaware of I Corps' change of front, exposed their flanks in the early afternoon to a potentially deadly thrust by that superbly self-confident force. But just at the instant that Franchet d'Esperey was about to

unleash it, news came from 51st Reserve Division, which had been left to hold the Meuse behind him, that it had lost a bridgehead to Hausen's Saxons and expected the collapse of the whole river line. Handling his corps brilliantly, d'Esperey turned it about, regained his old position, and launched a furious and successful counterattack.

The episode could not however restore the situation on the Meuse, and many of the crossing places fell into German hands that afternoon. Elsewhere too the circumstances of Fifth Army had deteriorated and that evening at eleven o'clock Lanrezac signalled, both to Joffre and his corps commanders, his intention of breaking off the action next day. 'Givet is threatened', he wrote, 'Namur taken. In view of this situation and the delay of the Fourth Army, I have decided to withdraw the army tomorrow on the front Beaumont-Givet'. The Great Retreat had begun.

On the road to Paris

The great retreat

Last to break contact with the Germans on the northern battlefront were the divisions of the British Expeditionary Force, which had fought on the Fifth Army's left at Mons throughout 23rd August. The action, though undoubtedly a part of that numerous series of engagements which the French call the Battle of the Frontiers, is often narrated by British military historians as if it were a completely separate affair. There are in fact some shreds of justification for such a treatment, for the spirit of co-operation displayed by the two commanders, Sir John French and Lanrezac, was a good deal less than it might and should have been. Lanrezac and French had not hit it off from the first; the former, who was an intellectual snob, thought the latter a fool; the latter, who was a class-bound cavalryman, thought the former no gentleman. Each had a little reason on his side. At their first meeting French, struggling gallantly, but unsuccessfully with the French language, asked Lanrezac why he thought the Germans had arrived at Huy (one of the major crossing points over the lower Meuse). Lanrezac told the interpreter to explain that he thought they had come there 'to fish'.

Cordial relations were never really re-established between the two men. On the day before the Battle of the Sambre, Lanrezac gave as his explanation for his failure to attack the advancing Germans the late arrival of the British who were still on the road from Maubege, the area in which they had concentrated after landing at Le Havre. On the evening of 23rd August, at the end of the Battle of the Sambre, he was to justify his withdrawal from the field by claiming that the British were in rear of his left flank which thus hung in the air and was vulnerable to envelopment.

In truth, at the moment that Lanrezac issued the order for retreat, the BEF was in position on the Fifth Army's left front, which it had held almost unyieldingly all day, and its commander was actually planning to

French

attack the following morning, so confident was he of his soldiers' superior fighting powers over those of the Germans opposite them.

They had been well demonstrated during the day. The British had arrived the evening previously and had dug themselves in along the line of the Condé Canal, which runs west-east through Mons to join the Meuse at Charleroi. The water obstacle is not a formidable one but cover was plentiful and fields of fire, where they could be found between the canal-side villages, are dead level, and so ideal for marksmen equipped with high velocity magazine rifles, as the British battalions were. The Lee-Enfield, a charger-loading weapon, holding ten .303-inch rounds, was sighted up to 1,000 yards, with a long distance sight calibrated up to 2,700 yards, its theoretical extreme range. In practice, British infantrymen were trained to engage targets at 600 yards, and to fire fifteen aimed rounds per minute. The battalion machine guns, two belt-fed Vickers guns, firing the infantry round at 500 a minute, would be deployed to the flanks. In hot engagement, therefore, each battalion on its 500-1,000 yard front could put down about 15,000 rounds of small arms fire in a minute.

Expertly delivered firepower was to be a vital ingredient of the BEF's resistance at Mons for it was attacked on the morning of Sunday 23rd August by overwhelming numbers. Kluck's First Army wheeling due south from Brussels (at Bülow's decision, taken in ignorance of the whereabouts of the BEF, and in the belief that Lanrezac's flank was exposed near Mons) arrived on the Condé Canal early that morning. He had four corps under command, from left to right, IV, III and IX, with II still on the line of march, and three cavalry divisions, 2nd, 4th and 9th. None were expecting to meet concerted resistance, for only two days before Kluck had been assured that as yet only small advance parties of British troops had landed in France. Thus, four British divisions, organised into two Corps, I under Haig and II under Smith-Dorrien, with a strong cavalry division under Allenby, had been assembled directly in the Germans' path without either enemy scouts or aviators detecting it.

It was Smith-Dorrien's II Corps that Kluck's soldiers were to fight on 23rd August, Haig's corps on the right of the front forming a refused flank which was echeloned back towards, though not in contact with, Lanrezac's left. The 5th and 3rd Divisions of II Corps stood on the left and right of Mons respectively, 3rd occupying a salient formed by a loop in the canal. Between 9 and 10 on the morning of 23rd August, after the German advance guards had made contact, their artillery began a brisk fire on the well defined line the British were holding and shortly afterwards the German infantry came on in close columns.

One of those who took part, Captain Walter Bloem, a distinguished novelist

Pontoon bridge across the Conde Canal near Mons built by engineers of the German 6th Division

*My message to the Troops of the Expeditionary
Force. Aug. 12th 1914*

• You are leaving home to fight for the safety
and honour of my Empire.

Belgium, whose country we are pledged to
defend, has been attacked and France is about to be
invaded by the same powerful foe.

I have implicit confidence in you my soldiers.
Duty is your watchword, and I know your duty will be
nobly done.

I shall follow your every movement with deepest
interest and mark with eager satisfaction your daily
progress, indeed your welfare will never be absent from
my thoughts.

I pray God to bless you and guard you and bring
you back victorious.

12th August. King George V's message to the troops of the BEF

THERE IS STILL A PLACE IN THE LINE FOR YOU

THIS SPACE IS RESERVED FOR A FIT MAN

Will you fill it?

Until 1915 there was little need for recruiting posters like this, for men came flocking in, thinking that the war might be over by Christmas

Haig

Smith-Dorrien

Allenby

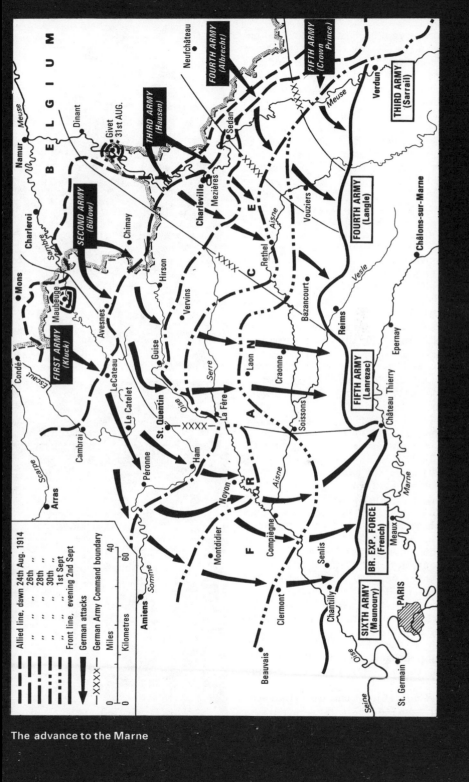

The advance to the Marne

and reserve officer of the 12th Grenadiers of the 5th Division, III Corps, led his company in this attack and has left a graphic account of the experience. After leading his company in short rushes across a broad expanse of meadow, he had reached some dead ground behind a low bank. His losses had been very heavy, 'but from now on the British fire gradually lessened, almost ceased. No hail of bullets greeted each rush forward, and we were able to get within 150 yards of the canal bank. I said, 'Now we'll do one more thirty-yard rush, all together, then fix bayonets and charge the houses and the canal banks. The enemy must have been waiting for this moment to get us all together at this range, for immediately the line rose it was if the hounds of hell had been loosed at us, yelling, barking, hammering as a mass of lead swept in among us . . . Voluntarily, and in many cases, involuntarily, we all collapsed flat on the grass as if swept by a scythe. From now on matters went from bad to worse. Wherever I looked, right or left, were dead or wounded . . . The worst was that the heaviest firing now began to come on us from the strip of wood . . . to our right rear. I blew my whistle full blast and any of the NCOs with whistles did the same. Still no good. The firing continued, more and more of my men being hit. [The fire, which Bloem thought was from a German machine gun, was in fact from one of the 1st East Surreys] I discovered too at this time that we had scarcely any ammunition left; and here we were isolated and 120 yards from the English positions.'

The greater number of Bloem's 160 men had been wounded or killed in this advance of just under 1,000 yards. And when at last he and the remnants struggled back, under cover of darkness, to battalion headquarters, he

Above right: British cavalry on the road south from Mons
Right: Soldiers of the 1st Scottish Rifles resting after the Battle of Mons

The Great Retreat — British troops
retire towards Le Cateau

found the commanding officer distraught. 'The battalion is all to pieces – my splendid battalion,' and the voice of this kindly, big-hearted man trembled as he spoke. 'I've given orders to entrench . . . will you see to that while the rest of the companies get re-organised? Watch the front very carefully. If the British have the slightest suspicion of the condition we are in, they will counterattack tonight and send us all to glory.'

The arrival late that evening at Sir John French's headquarters at Le Cateau of the young Edward Spears, liaison officer between the BEF and the Fifth Army, with news that Lanrezac had ordered a retreat, dashed all British hopes of launching such a counterattack, even if they had been realistic. Instead, on the following morning, II Corps, flanked by I Corps, which had scarcely been engaged, broke contact with the enemy and began the march southward. Mons had not been a victory, though many patriotic writers tried then and later to make it appear so; on one position of the front, in the salient north of Mons, the 3rd Division had been forced to yield ground. Yet it was certainly not a defeat. It is best thought of as a successful delaying action which also assured the security of the Fifth Army's left flank at a moment of desperate crisis.

The BEF now joined the Fifth and Fourth Armies in retreat. Whither they were to retire, none knew on the morning of 24th August, not even Joffre himself as yet. That day was given over by him to a re-appraisal of his strategy. On the next, 25th August, he issued to his armies the second General Instruction of the campaign, a splendidly succinct document which devoted the barest space to acknowledging the failure of the offensive ordered in General Instruction No 1, and then proceeded briskly to outline his plans for the next offensive phase. Its most important paragraph ran:

'Future operations will be conducted in such a way as to reconstruct on our

Above: Horse lines of a German cavalry regiment encamped during the advance from Belgium
Right: A German telephone section. Poor communications badly hampered the German command

left a force capable of resuming the offensive by a combination of the Fourth and Fifth Armies, the British army and new forces drawn from the east, while the other armies hold the enemy in check for such time as may be necessary.

'Each of the Third, Fourth and Fifth Armies, during its retreat, will take account of the movement of the neighbouring armies, with which they must remain in liaison. The movement will be covered by rear-guards, left at favourable points . . . to halt the enemy's march, or, at any rate, to delay it by short and violent counterattacks in which the artillery will be the principal element employed.

'Before Amiens . . . or behind the Somme . . . a new group of forces will

Above: A contemporary British war artist's conception of the Battle of Le Cateau. It bore no relation to reality
Below: A German skirmishing line in France
Right: An order group of the 1st Scottish Rifles before Le Cateau, 25th August 1914

British, French and Belgian officers
en route for a German POW camp

Victorious (but by now tired) German troops man temporary trenches

be constituted by elements transported by rail (VII Corps, four reserve divisions and perhaps another Active army corps) between 27th August and 2nd September. This group will be ready to take the offensive in the general direction of St Pol-Arras or Arras-Bapaume.'

This document, which reached the French armies on 26th August, was a remarkable and vital one, for it decreed both the fashion in which the retreat would be conducted and the creation of the force which would intervene to bring it to an end. To be called the Sixth Army, and commanded by General Maunoury, it was to be formed by transferring divisions from the French right wing in Lorraine along the railway lines which run from Toul and Nancy to Paris. For the French, in retreating, had the good luck to be pulling back on an intact communication system, of which they were to make excellent use – and never more so than in the creation of the Sixth Army. The Germans, on the contrary, were advancing across country in which the communication system had been devastated. That held true not only for the railways, of which they were not to be able to make full use until late September, but also of the telephone network. As a result, liaison between German headquarters and the fighting front was to be severely hampered. Ironically, much of the damage to the telephone system was wrought by marauding German cavalrymen who imagined that, in chopping down the posts or slashing the wires, they were in some way hindering the French commanders' handling of their units.

The counterattacks and delaying actions which Joffre decreed should be fought had begun even before his General Instruction No 2 had reached the armies. The first was fought by Smith-Dorrien's II Corps at Le Cateau on 26th August in a desperate attempt to disengage Kluck's infantry who were clinging so tenaciously to its line of retreat. Smith-Dorrien's situation was not a comfortable one for the enemy were in superior strength and Haig, whose corps had played the lesser part at Mons, had taken fright after a German night attack at Landrecies the night before and was now prudently leading it southward on the far side of the Forest of Mormal. II Corps was thus left to fight alone on an awkward front on ground commanded by the enemy over which he played a powerful artillery onto the British lines from the beginning of the battle. It made all this more telling practice since the British artillery commander, in order to put heart into the infantry, ordered his own guns to leave their covered positions and take post in the open, in full view of friend and enemy alike.

As a result the corps, which had lost heavily in the preceding day of retreat, as well as bearing the brunt of the losses at Mons, again suffered serious casualties. This was particularly so on the right flank, that which Haig had left uncovered by his uncomradely withdrawal: its units were saved from destruction only by a tricky disengagement. On the left, where the situation grew similarly perilous, the arrival of Sordet's Cavalry Corps, full of fight, despite its dispiriting pursuit of shadows during the previous fortnight, relieved the pressure and the whole of II Corps, minus many of its guns and a dolefully large proportion of its infantry, was eventually enabled to get clear. Its centre had held throughout the action and, as had the wings, had inflicted heavy losses on the attacking German infantry.

De Langle de Cary's Fourth Army, which had fallen back after its disastrous foray into the Ardennes to its original positions across the Meuse, was also heavily engaged on 26th August in defence of the crossing-places against the German Fourth Army. Fighting in familiar territory its divisions were almost everywhere successful in repelling the enemy, whom they were not to allow to cross until 29th August.

While de Langle was fully stretched on the Meuse, Lanrezac, still prophesying disaster but preening himself meanwhile, was being prodded by Joffre to organise a counter-stroke. The French Commander-in-Chief, besides wishing for such a counter-stroke in principle, was also concerned to relieve German pressure on the BEF whose commander had, on 26th August, revealed to him in a highly emotional way his fears for the safety of his force and his desire to rest it from active operations. Joffre had accordingly ordered Lanrezac to use the line of the Somme and the Oise, between Guise and St Quentin, as a stop line from which to launch a counterattack against the oncoming Germans. In this way he hoped to disengage the BEF (and also afford Sixth Army time to concentrate on the left flank). Lanrezac showed himself not merely unwilling but insolently ill-disposed to carry out these wishes of the Commander-in-Chief and it took a personal visit from Joffre, on the morning of 28th August, to bring him to heel. The visit was notable on two accounts: it marked the moment when Joffre lost confidence in Lanrezac – and if it is thought that Lanrezac had been indulged over long, it should be remembered that his pre-war prestige as a teacher of strategy was higher perhaps than that of any other officer in the French army; and it gave rise to one of the few displays of temper into which Joffre fell throughout the course of the campaign. Joffre subscribed very strongly to the view, which the elder Moltke had done perhaps most to propagate but to which almost all great commanders have subscribed, that a general must above all else retain his calm; his own outbursts of temper or excitement not only hinder his own clearness of judgement, they also sap the con-

Galliéni

fidence of his staff. Joffre's monumental calm was legendary. But on this occasion he angrily reproved Lanrezac for his insubordination, threatened him with dismissal and decided to return the day following to see his orders carried out.

Lanrezac issued overnight the necessary instructions but held himself almost completely aloof from the direction of the ensuing battle. It developed therefore in an ill coordinated fashion, the Germans managing to push the French out of their positions on the western flank of the battlefront, but suffering a serious check to their opposite wing. There the Guard Corps, in an advance reminiscent of that they had made forty years earlier at St Privat, drove a series of assaults against French positions on the high ground around Guise and after suffering heavy losses were brought to a standstill. The commander of the 1st Foot Guards (*Erste Garde Regiment zu Fuss*), the premier regiment of the Prussian army, whose tall, brass-mitre caps were as distinctive a feature of the peacetime Berlin scene as the Grena-

diers' bearskins of London's, then went forward. He was Prince Eitel Frederick, the Kaiser's second son, and his appearance in the front rank, banging a regimental drum he had seized from a bandsman, was stirring enough to regenerate the guardsmen's fighting spirit, and carry them forward onto the enemy's positions (which he was then found to have abandoned).

The battle at this stage was going badly for the French on both flanks. But at one o'clock the commander of Lanrezac's as yet disengaged I Corps, General Franchet d'Esperey ('Desperate Frankie' to the BEF), at last extracted permission from Lanrezac to intervene. He decided to do so in flamboyant style, calling foward the regimental bands and colour parties and placing himself on a chestnut horse in the midst of his men. The deployment of his units took time and it was not until six in the evening that they appeared in strength in the gap between the hard-pressed X and III Corps, but when they did so, supported by the massed batteries of the corps and divisional artilleries, the spirit of the whole French line of battle was aroused and it moved irresistably forward to recover most of the ground it had lost during the day. De Langle looked forward to re-crossing the Oise on the following day.

But on 30th August, as for the six previous days, the orders were for retreat again. Joffre had hoped to stand and fight on the Oise-Somme line as Castelnau was doing so splendidly on the line of the Moselle at Nancy. But the assembly of Maunoury's Sixth Army was not proceeding as swiftly as he had hoped and the commander of the BEF was showing himself more and more reluctant to stay with the French right wing. His eyes were now fixed on St Nazaire on the Atlantic coast, which had been re-designated the BEFs main base. Joffre was compelled therefore to defer his order to halt and face

Poincaré

'facts, distances and place-names'. 'Briefly,' announced Galliéni, 'you may expect the German armies to be before the walls of Paris in twelve days.' That evening, Messimy, having dismissed the unfortunate Michel from the military governorship of the city, pressed it upon Galliéni, 'Shaking my hand several times' when he accepted, Galliéni recorded, and 'even kissing me' so that he gathered 'that the place I was succeeding to was not an enviable one.' How unenviable, a census of the garrison was shortly to reveal. The 61st and 62nd Reserve Divisions, which should have been available, had been spirited away into the Zone of the Armies, from which even President Poincaré lacked the constitutional power to recall them. This left him with only a single first-line division, the 45th, which was raised from among the white settlers of the North African XIX Military District and had been detained in Paris while moving to the battlefront by train. On 28th August, Galliéni's powers were increased when the Zone of the Armies was extended to include Paris, which brought the civil government of the city under his control and allowed him to decree a sweeping programme of military preparations. It entailed the destruction of buildings and woodland wherever fields of fire were obstructed, the demolition of bridges and the barricading of roads. The city was hastily stocked with grain and livestock which was put to graze in the parks. At the turn of the month, the city passed even more completely under military control, the government, which had been reconstituted on 26th August, deciding to depart for Bordeaux on 30th August (as it in fact did on 2nd September).

about, which would in consequence have to be given when the armies had approached considerably nearer to Paris.

The safety of Paris, which was not Joffre's immediate concern since it lay outside the Zone of the Armies, had now become almost the principal preoccupation of the government. The 'entrenched camp', whose strength had so dispirited Schlieffen, turned out, upon inspection by the general of engineers whom Messimy had appointed to refurbish the works, to be a good deal less ready for defence than it should. Most alarmingly, it almost lacked defenders. Counting his garrison on 25th August, Messimy found only one cavalry division, four divisions of Territorials (the oldest class of reservists) and some cadres at the depots.

He sent at once for help to Galliéni, the conqueror of Madagascar, who would have replaced Michel in 1911 had he not demanded a free hand in the appointment of officers, which no Republican government would grant. Galliéni pored with him over Joffre's General Instruction No 2, looking for

Another advantage, from Galliéni's viewpoint, of the city's inclusion in the Zone of the Armies was that Joffre now felt readier to station fighting formations within its defended perimeter. As a result, he returned the 61st and 62nd Reserve

133

Asquith

Kitchener

Soldiers of the Queen's Bays with prisoners of the Death's Head Hussars after Nery

ivisions (not before they had been
mauled in a clash with Kluck's oncoming army, added another Terri-
torial division and two brigades of
marines and, more important, subordinated Maunoury's Sixth Army to
alliéni. The disadvantage was that
e too now became a subordinate of
offre, whom he disliked.

Another issue of command had been
settled during the same period: that
f Sir John French's relationship
ith the French high command. The
ritish government, having impressed
pon him both the necessity of safe-
uarding his army from extreme risk
nd his right to disregard Joffre's
uggestions if they should imperil it,
as now itself disturbed by the Field-
Marshal's apparent desire to divorce
is operations from those of the
rench and put the BEF temporarily
ut of harm's way, a departure which
ad stimulated the most protests
om Paris. On 31st August, Asquith
ecided that Field-Marshal Kitchener,
he new Minister of War, must leave

to confront French immediately.

The communications which had so
alarmed Asquith and Kitchener had
been sent by French on 30th August
and read: 'My confidence in the ability
of the leaders of the French army to
carry this campaign to a successful
conclusion is fast waning, and this is
my real reason for the decision I have
taken to move the British forces so far
back. [He had announced that he was
withdrawing them south of the Seine]
I have been pressed very hard to
remain [by Joffre, in particular, at a
meeting on 29th August at Compiègne],
even in my shattered condition in the
fighting line, but have absolutely
refused to do so, and I hope you will
approve of the course I have taken.'
Kitchener would not, on four main
grounds. First, he knew that many
French formations had suffered far
worse than the BEF (French losses for
the five months of 1914 were to total
400,000 *killed,* of which the majority

Belgian refugees arrive in Paris

135

were suffered in August and September); second, he was determined to deny French the reinforcements he was demanding, since he needed them for the formation of the 'Kitchener' armies; third, he believed in the alliance and believed too that it could only be maintained by the BEF bearing its fair share of sacrifice; fourth, he rightly feared that unless the BEF kept its place in the line, the Germans would break through it and destroy the French armies. Thus, though he and French were on amiable terms, he conducted their interview in Paris on 1st September with severity and ended it only when he had impressed on French that although he did not expect him to expose the BEF to risk of envelopment (as French felt it had been left exposed at Mons and Le Cateau) he was to keep his place in line and co-operate willingly in Joffre's strategic designs.

While this interview was proceeding, the BEF had been fighting a series of skilful rearguard actions, at Crépy-en-Vallois, at Villers-Cotterets and, a famous engagement, at Néry. There L Battery, Royal Horse Artillery, supporting the 1st Cavalry Brigade, had been drawn into a duel with the whole artillery of the German 4th Cavalry Divison. Its guns had been knocked out one by one until only a single 13-pounder had been left to cover the 1st Cavalry Brigade's and 4th Division's withdrawal. Its crew too was eventually disabled but by then the British rearguards had got away, while the 4th Cavalry Division had been so badly cut up in the action that it was not to play any active rôle in the campaign for the next week.

To overcome delaying actions of this sort, often very bitterly contested, had been the daily experience of German units now for nine days during which the mere covering of distance had been the ordeal enough. Many of Kluck's soldiers had done 150 miles on foot before crossing the Belgian frontier into France. They had since come a further hundred miles as the crow flies, many more if their meanderings are measured on a road map. Bloem describes the effect this gruelling march had had:

'For three whole weeks, ever since we detrained at Elsdorf on 10th August we had not had a single rest day. Day after day onwards without ceasing every night a fresh billet . . . Before the war I should have regarded such power of endurance as beyond the capacity of the most robust peasant lads . . . how the men's feet suffered. From time to time we had to examine them; and it was no pleasure to look at the inflamed heels, soles and toes of my wretched young lads, whole patches of skin rubbed off to the raw flesh. Many a morning the company commanders would ride up to the bat

The dusty road to Paris

talion commander (as field officers, all would be mounted): Major, could you explain to the higher command the need for a rest day? The men literally can go no further . . . 'Gentlemen, I assure you I know all that as well as you . . . Apparently, this frantic, everlasting onward rush is absolutely essential, and so you must keep on taking every care of your men on the march and use all your powers to keep up their spirits at any price. Make it clear to them, that we must allow the enemy no rest until we have utterly defeated him on the whole front. Tell them that sweat is saving blood.'

Two days after making this diary entry, Bloem led his men past a village signpost reading: Paris 50 kilometres. 'Now we were only thirty miles from the City of Light,' he wrote, 'thirty miles, that meant two day's march at most at our present rate of progress; so that by tomorrow evening at latest we would be standing at its gates, and perhaps the following morning, make our triumphal entry into the surrendered city.'

The following day, on which Bloem hoped to find himself at the gates of Paris, would be 2nd September, to every German Sedan Day, the great national celebration of Prussia's victory over the French forty-four years before. Every German heart was now set on seeing that victory repeated on a magnified scale. Only at Moltke's field headquarters did any doubt exist as to the outcome of this brilliant campaign. But there the doubts had become persistent and were growing in intensity.

The miracle of the Marne

The course of the campaign had, by the third week, already begun to bear out Schlieffen's dictum, itself an encapsulation of an older wisdom, that 'the power of the attacker diminishes as he advances'. Moltke, who had begun to display again all those signs of nervousness and pessimism which had so alarmed his staff during mobilisation and which would become quite overwhelming by the end of the campaign, now found himself as he approached the crisis a good deal shorter of troops than he had been at the outset. One corps (III Reserve) had been left outside Antwerp, to watch the Belgian army; VII Reserve Corps and one brigade of VII had been left to besiege Maubeuge (which was not to fall until after the battle of the Marne); another brigade of IV Reserve Corps had been left to garrison Brussels; 24th Reserve Division was besieging the little fortress of Charlemont at Givet, garrisoned by only 3,500 Territorials – as stout a body of men as France put into the field that summer; most important of all, two corps, XI and the Guard Reserve, had been withdrawn from the west and transferred to the eastern front, in anticipation of further Russian successes in East Prussia.

The great victory of Tannenberg (30th August) extinguished all fears for the safety of East Prussia but did not lead to the return of the transferred corps. Thus Moltke, who had counted the equivalent of seventy-five divisions in his order of battle in the first week of August, now disposed of only sixty-seven, while the Allies' strength, including the four Belgian divisions besieged in Antwerp, now stood at seventy-nine.

Despite this imbalance, whose effect had not yet become apparent, for the good reason that the Allies, while in retreat, could not make felt their superiority in numbers, was still – indeed now more than ever – intent upon bringing the Schlieffen plan to a triumphant conclusion. At the insistance of Prince Rupprecht's staff, he

had given permission for the Sixth and Seventh Armies to resume their counteroffensive in Lorraine and, despite the setback imposed on them by Castelnau's spirited action at the Grand Couronné (22nd-27th August), he was disposed to consent to Rupprecht's notion of achieving a double envelopment of the French army, by continuing to push for a breakthrough in Lorraine.

On the right or western wing of the front, he had, on 27th August, faced the dilemma which had defeated Schlieffen – the 'problem of Paris' – and solved it by ignoring its existence. He had, without apparent difficulty, decided that Kluck, whom he now released from subordination to Bülow, should pass to the west of Paris, while Bülow's Second Army should direct its axis of advance on Paris itself. The army commanders responded to this order individually on 20th August but in such a fashion as to prompt Moltke to modify it considerably.

The Duke of Württemberg, commanding Fourth Army, reporting that he had at last driven de Langle's Fourth Army off the Meuse crossings (de Langle had in fact abandoned them in order to follow the general retreat) suggested that he profit from this success by advancing due south instead of rather south-west as Moltke's 7th August directive had laid down. Hausen, commanding Third Army, proposed at the same time that he also shift his axis of advance due south in order to march in parallel with the Fourth. Meanwhile Bülow reporting a complete success at St Quentin-Guise, asked and was given permission to pursue Lanrezac's Fifth Army due southward also, and made the suggestion, to which Kluck concurred, that First Army should turn to the south-east, that is through ninety degrees from the axis Moltke had originally ordered it to take in order to pass to the west of Paris, and seek to cut off the retreat of Fifth Army to the Marne. With all these

Landsturm guarding Russian prisoners captured at Tannenberg

proposals, to which he was able to respond by wireless, Moltke agreed.

Kluck is often accused of 'dis - obedience' in moving to march on Bülow's flank rather than in continuing to pass to the west of Paris but it is difficult to see how that charge can be framed convincingly. Had he continued on a south-westerly course, the fear which had haunted Schlieffen would certainly have been realised. Maunoury would have sallied out of the entrenched camp and, taking him in flank, probably defeated him, certainly have imposed a fatal delay on his advance. As it was, serious gaps had already begun to open between the three right wing armies and their neighbours: by 30th August twenty miles between Kluck and Bülow, twenty miles between Bülow and Hausen and about fifteen miles between Hausen and Württemberg.

French General Headquarters, plotting the onset of the German battle line on its large scale map from hour to hour, was now seeking to gauge when and where the counter-stroke should be delivered. It could not be much further delayed, for if the Germans were to advance beyond the Seine, the garrisons of two strong fortress flanks of the French front, Paris on the left, Verdun on the right, would lose contact with the field army and the whole French fighting line fall into disarray. Clearly battle would have to be delivered somewhere between the Marne and its tributaries, the Petit Morin and Grand Morin; while Maunoury's front of attack would lie on the Ourcq, which flows south into the Marne thirty miles east of Paris.

Joffre had done much already to prepare for the coming counterstroke. On 3rd September, exasperated beyond repair with Lanrezac's pessimism and prevarication, he removed him summarily from command and replaced him with the victor of

141

Above: Belgian soldiers defending Antwerp
Below: Belgian cavalry falling back on Antwerp

Above: A Belgian roadblock outside Antwerp
Below: A defended barricade across a Belgian road

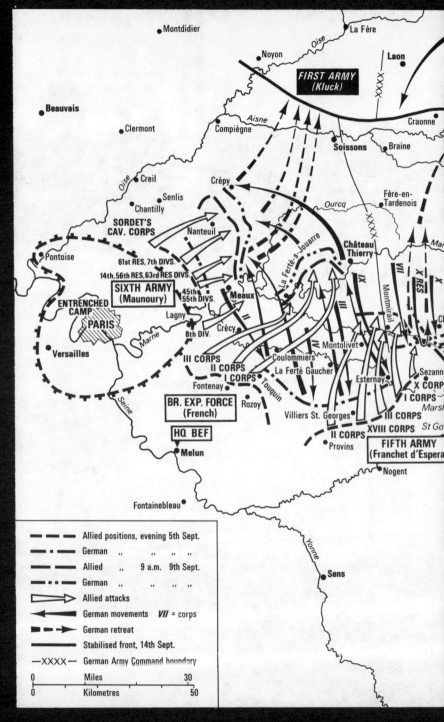

The Battle of the Marne and the Retreat to the Aisne

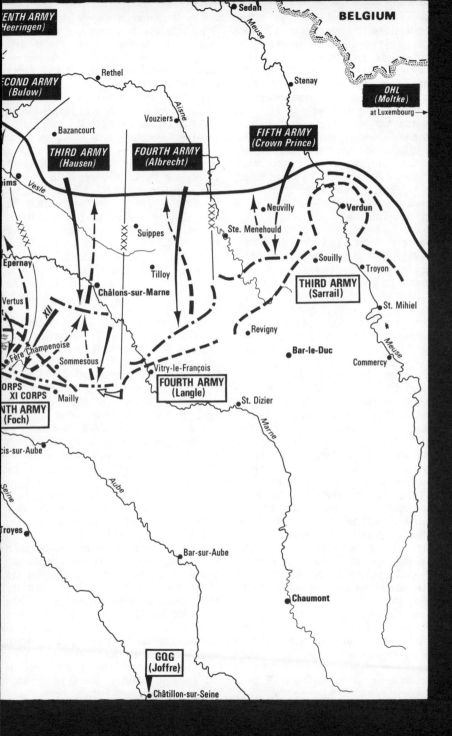

Guise, Franchet d'Esperey. That stout-hearted warrior demonstrated the spirit in which he proposed to exercise his new command within the first minutes of assuming it. His Chief of Staff, who he overheard placating a corps commander on the telephone, was asked why the conversation was going on so long. Told that the general was explaining 'the difficulties he finds in carrying out the orders he has received', Franchet d'Esperey took the receiver: 'You've received an order. It must be carried out. From now on the word is: march or croak'.

Joffre had also promoted another fire-eater, Ferdinand Foch, whose XX Corps had saved the day at Morhange during the German counter-offensive in Lorraine on 21st August. De Langle's Third Army having proved too large to handle easily, Joffre had detached its left wing, re-named it the Ninth Army and given it to Foch. It was to play a crucial role in the coming battle. At the same time, Joffre was busy transferring divisions to the left of his array from the right which, though it could ill spare them was now committed to a static rôle in fortified positions on the Moselle. By 5th September, the Sixth Army (Maunoury) would have grown to three cavalry divisions, two Active divisions and three Reserve divisions; the Fifth Army had been reinforced by two cavalry divisions; the Ninth Army (Foch), originally consisting of four Active, two Reserve and one cavalry divisions, was reinforced by another two Active divisions. Four other Active divisions were on their way by 5th September.

Moltke, who had transferred his headquarters from Koblenz to Luxembourg on 29th August, as near as he was to approach to the battlefront during the campaign, had become aware of the general outline of Joffre's redispositions and was growing more and more uneasy at its impact. The 'problem of Paris' which Kluck still

quite disregarded as he himself had done hitherto had begun to bulk very large in his thoughts. As he saw very clearly, the continual French retirement exposed the flank of the great right wheel to an attack from *Festung Paris*. On 2nd September, therefore, he modified his orders of 27th August and 30th, directing Kluck while maintaining the same axis of advance, to follow Bülow in echelon which meant to his right rear. There were several reasons why this order was unwelcome to Kluck. The first was that he bitterly resented the notion that he should act merely as Bülow's flank guard; the second, that having clung like death to the heels of the Fifth Army, he was now rather in advance of Bülow; and thus, third, in order to comply with Moltke's new order, he would have to give up ground already won.

Two days later on 4th September, Moltke's picture of the situation had crystallised further. He now anticipated that the threat from Paris would be the most serious with which he would have to contend and that the victory, a belief to which he still clung, would be won east of the upper Marne, between Reims and Verdun, by the Fourth and Fifth Armies. They accordingly were to shift their axes of advance from the south to south-east, in order to coordinate a pincer movement with Sixth and Seventh Armies against Castelnau's and Dubail's armies on the Moselle. Accordingly both Second and First Armies were to adopt a defensive posture against the threat from Paris, Second swinging on its right to face west, First actually retracing its steps across the Marne in order to fill the gap between the Marne and Oise, also facing west. Kluck received these orders with incredulity. He had been so fully occupied during the last week of advance in driving his subordinates forward, refusing them rest and forcing them to overcome every check whatever the cost, that he had had

Falkenhayn

no time to question what underlay the confident communiques issued by OHL, let alone establish the truth himself. Falkenhayn (the Prussian Minister of War), who had visited the headquarters of the German Crown Prince, the Duke of Württemberg and von Hausen on 1st September, had guessed at the facts. 'It isn't a battle won, it's an orderly retreat', he had told Moltke, 'Show me your trophies and your prisoners' (which were far fewer than a truly victorious army would have captured). But Kluck, for over a month, had had his eyes fixed only on his own front of advance, and had believed that the campaign was approaching a triumphant culmination in the envelopment of the French right wing, and was now bitterly surprised to discover that OHL had, without explanation, abandoned the Schlieffen plan and now wish to consign him to a secondary rôle.

These orders reached him on 5th September, which left him little time to take up the precautionary positions Moltke had ordered, in view at any rate of what was happening at GQG.

For there, the day before, Joffre had come to his momentous decision. A long debate between the mandarins of the general staff had preceded it. Berthelot, the Chief of the Operations Section, had been for postponing a counter-offensive until Kluck had penetrated further across the Paris-Verdun line; Gamelin, Joffre's Chef du Cabinet (Private Office), spoke for a group, whose opinions Maunoury and Galliéni shared, who wanted to see Kluck and the German right wing assailed at once. Joffre, as was his wont, had listened impassively to the debate. Then he had taken measures to secure the advice of his commanders in the field: to Foch he had sent an envoy, to d'Esperey a telegram asking if he would be ready to attack on the morrow, to Galliéni a request to seek the co-operation of Field-Marshal French in an advance against the German left wing.

Of the replies he received, that from Franchet d'Esperey most impressed him. Paquette, who had seen Foch, merely brought back word that he would be ready to attack on 6th September. Galliéni, who had been to French to ascertain his willingness to join in the battle, subsequently claimed that he, in a telephone conversation reporting his findings to Joffre, successfully urged him to move over at once to the offensive. Whatever the truth of that – and it is one of the most vigorously argued controversies of the history of the Marne, though Joffre always affected to misunderstand what all the fuss was about – he seems at the time to have been genuinely excited by Franchet d'Esperey's reply and not so by Galliéni's. What d'Esperey, who had been to see Sir John French on his own initiative that afternoon, had written was: 'The battle cannot take place until the day after tomorrow, the 6th... The following are necessary for the success of the operation. 1. Close and absolute co-operation from the Sixth Army . . . It must reach the Ourcq tomorrow, 5th Sep-

Above: German infantry at the beginning of their last marches towards the Marne
Below: A section of a French field battery following up the German retreat after the Marne. The village is Chauconier, near Meaux

Above: The 1st Cameronians, BEF, receive rations during the Battle of the Marne, 8th September
Below: French cuirassiers escort German prisoners taken at the Marne

Above: A British Avro 504 flown on reconnaissance during the campaign
Below: A German LVG two-seater under guard at Belfort, September 1914

tember. If not, the British will not march. 2. My Army can fight on the 6th, but is not in brilliant condition ... 3. It would furthermore be well for Foch's detachment to participate vigorously in the action in the direction of Montmort.'

'With that intelligent audacity, that is found only in the souls of great leaders', Joffre wrote afterwards, 'Franchet d'Esperey splendidly seized the situation and did not hesitate to answer 'YES' to a question that would have caused most men to flinch.' That evening Belin, the Chief of Joffre's Staff, issued the orders for the coming battle, General Instruction No 6. 'It is desirable to take advantage of the exposed position of the German First Army to concentrate against it the strength of the Allied left wing armies . . . With a view to launching an attack on the 6th. The dispositions completed on the evening of 5th September will be:

'Sixth Army . . . ready to cross the Ourcq . . . to the general direction of Château Thierry . . . The British army . . . facing east, ready to attack in the general direction on Montmirail . . . The Fifth Army . . . ready to attack from south to north . . . The Ninth Army . . . will cover the right of the Fifth Army, holding the boundaries of the Marshes of St Gond.'

On the morning of 5th September, the leading units of Maunoury's Sixth Army began their march eastward to their allotted forming up positions on the banks of the Ourcq. The march was intended and expected to be a peaceful manoeuvre, it not being thought that the enemy would be encountered until the river line was reached. It was with dismay and surprise, therefore, that the leading formations, the 55th and 56th Reserve Divisions, reacted to the shell-fire which dropped among their scattered ranks during the midday break. Hastily recalled to arms, the columns formed up and raced forward to clear the Germans off the low range of

wooded heights which stood between them and their objective.

This well organised surprise had been brought about as the result of intelligent perception of the way events were moving by the commander of the only sizeable German force in the area, von Gronau of the IV Reserve Corps. It was as a result of a suspicion rather than of concrete Intelligence reports that he had formed the impression that the French were moving towards his flank that morning (his corps was in column of route) but his impression was a very strong one and, telling his Chief of Staff, Colonel von der Heydt (whose descendant was to lead a parachute battalion in the attack on Crete thirty years later) that delay would be fatal, he ordered his two divisions to face right and the divisional artilleries to open fire into the valley below.

The resulting shellfire may be regarded as the opening shots of the Battle of the Marne, delivered almost twenty-four hours earlier than Joffre had intended. This premature outbreak was to have an influential effect on the course of the battle, for if Gronau had not scented danger and acted to avert it, Kluck would have pressed onward into the trap; Gronau's IV Reserve Corps was in fact following in the wake of Kluck's advance when he faced it westward.

Kluck's immediate reaction to the first news of the situation was to despatch one of his advancing corps, II, from the Morin to the Ourcq to help Gronau, who had decided that his successful attack would be bound to attract a stronger riposte than he could sustain and that an ordered retreat was now his best policy. During the course of the next two days, 6th–7th September, Kluck was to engage one after another of his corps as the tide of battle swelled along the Ourcq, detaching each in turn from the battle line along the Morin to switch it northwards, along the rear of his engaged divisions on

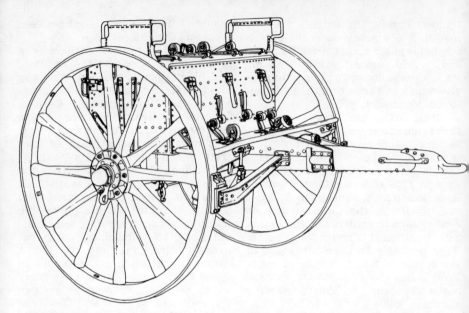

The Allies, unlike the Central Powers, foresaw no need for super-heavy guns in the impending war, as they were convinced that the war would be short and very mobile. For this sort of war, light manoeuvrable guns were what were needed, and the British 18-pounder fitted admirably into this category. An excellent gun of its type, it was easily moved, accurate and well-liked by its crews. In the early stages of the war, it proved invaluable in the way foreseen, though the Allies were retreating

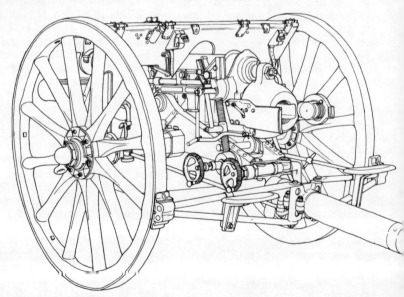

A British 18-pounder Field Battery in action 8th September during the Battle of the Marne

rather than advancing as envisaged. But when the war settled down to trench fighting rather than manoeuvre, light field guns proved to be of limited use, for their indirect fire was what was needed in the new circumstances, and this sort of fire was not the forte of the 18-pounder. *Calibre:* 3.3-inches. *Barrel length:* 28 calibres. *Weight of shell:* 18 pounds. *Weight of gun and carriage:* 3,800 pounds. *Range:* 7,000 yards. *Elevation:* —5° to +16°. The limber for the 18-pounder, as for all other light field pieces, was designed to steady the gun when the two parts were linked together for travelling, as well as providing storage for such tools as were needed for light repairs on the gun and ready ammunition should the gun go into action before the supply column could provide it with shells. When in motion, the gun and limber were much steadier as a four-wheel rather than two two-wheel vehicles, and allowed the crew to ride on the limber. On going into action, the gun could be unlimbered quickly and turned to fire on the enemy while the limber and horses were taken back a little to a position of comparative safety.

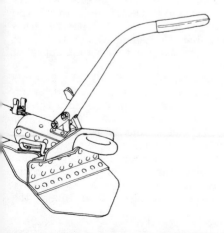

the Ourcq to the right flank. What began as a defensive measure, forced on him by the need to prevent Maunoury outflanking him and rolling up the whole German right wing, gathered momentum so successfully that by the morning of 7th September Kluck had convinced himself that he had the chance, was indeed on the point of defeating Maunoury. Accordingly he decided upon the extremely risky move of IX Corps from the right of Bülow's Second Army to the right of his own. He did so in the knowledge that this would open an unbridgeable gap between his and Bülow's fronts but in the belief that the BEF, which he knew to be opposite it, would take no profit from the opportunity this offered, since it or its commander, perhaps both, had lost the will to fight.

It had been a precondition of Joffre's decision to manoeuvre for the counterattack, however, to assure himself of Sir John's willingness to fight, which he had done in a personal visit, during which he declared that 'the honour of England is at stake'. French, however strongly deterred by prudence, had promised to play his part. Accordingly he, with d'Esperey's much larger Fifth Army, had turned about and on the evening of 6th September was advancing to contact with Bülow's Second Army on the Grand Morin.

The order to reverse direction was received with enthusiasm in d'Esperey's army and his four corps assaulted sharply whenever they met Germans on the morning of 6th September. Those they met, however, were mainly advance guards who did not resist stiffly so that by the end of the day the Fifth Army had won back a good deal of ground very cheaply. These gains had been assisted by Bülow's tactical decision to withdraw troops into reserve against the danger of a deterioration of the situation on Kluck's front. On the following day the whole of Fifth Army

again made ground against a retreating enemy and on 8th September de Maud'huy's I Corps broke the resistance of the German VII Corps, on Bülow's right, and turned his line. This effectively secured the flank of the gap into which the BEF was advancing and threatened the very greatest danger to the Kluck-Bülow wing.

Two factors were to rescue them from complete disaster: the comparative caution of the BEF's advance and the intemperate aggressiveness of Foch, commanding Ninth Army in the Marshes of St Gond. The BEF, starting from positions twelve miles further south than Joffre had envisaged they would, took consonantly longer to make contact with the Germans than d'Esperey's units. And though opposed only by the cavalry divisions of von der Marwitz's corps, and their attached *Jägers*, they made only very slow progress thereafter. Indeed, laudable though it was of French to take the risk of inserting his force into the gap between Kluck and Bülow, his lack of boldness thereafter robbed his deed of much of its virtue. Even so, the position he had reached on 8th September, on the south bank of the Marne, was one which could be decisively exploited, if d'Esperey could transfer sufficient men to reinforce him.

Unfortunately, d'Esperey, though unaware of the opportunity which French's advance offered, was more concerned at that moment with the plight of Foch, who having been ordered to defend the Marshes of St Gond against very strong opposing forces – the left wing of Bülow's Second Army and all of Hausen's Third – had chosen to do so in characteristically vigorous fashion. During two days of constant combat, his army had gradually been sapped of fighting strength and on the morning of 9th September d'Esperey decided to side-step two of his four corps towards Foch in order to relieve pressure on him. Accordingly the

Above: A pontoon bridge over the Marne built by Royal Engineers at La Ferte sous Jouarre, 8th September 1914
Below: German dead in a field near Lizy after the Battle of the Marne

troops who might have moved to help the BEF exploit the gap between Kluck and Bülow did not arrive until too late and then in little strength. So that the British though they had reached the Marne on 8th September and began to cross it on 9th September did not deliver the fatal blow that they might have done if reinforced at the crucial moment.

By the time the British began to cross the Marne, and as Rupprecht's second attempt on the Grand Couronné was flickering out in failure, the result of the battle of the Marne had already been decided and in a way which bore out all those philosophical and psychological interpretations of the nature of war in which the professors at the French Staff College, Foch foremost among them, had been given to delight. Foch, paraphrasing the words of the 19th century political thinker de Maistre, used to argue that 'a battle won is a battle that one refuses to admit is lost'. On 9th September, the German General Headquarters

Above: German Jägers under guard after the Marne
Right: French dragoons with German prisoners and booty

decided that the Marne was a lost battle. They arrived at their decision in the most bizarre fashion.

Communication between OHL, even when it had moved to Luxembourg, and the field armies had been slow and erratic throughout the campaign. The telephone network was inadequate and often broken and, although OHL and each of the seven army headquarters was equipped with wireless, the sets were primitive and affected by jamming from a powerful French transmitter broadcasting from the Eiffel Tower. Denied a clear picture of the way the battle was progressing, Moltke accordingly decided, on the morning of 8th September, after a long situation conference with his strategic advisers, to send the head of his Intelligence section, Lieutenant-Colonel Hentsch, on a round tour of the right wing army head-quarters, from the Fifth to the First, in order to gather information but also, if necessary, to co-ordinate a retreat if one had already been under-taken. Accordingly at eleven Hentsch set off by car on his long drive. From the Duke of Württemberg's head-quarters he telephoned Luxembourg to report the situation on Fifth and Fourth Armies' fronts satisfactory; both were making progress against Sarrail's Third Army. Later in the day he telephoned from von Hausen's headquarters 'situation and point of view entirely favourable at Third Army'. Late in the day he reached Bülow's headquarters but by night all that had reached Moltke at Luxem-bourg was the cryptic message 'Situ-ation serious but not desperate at Second Army'.

This radiogram was the outcome of a meeting which had occupied the whole evening and which had ended with the agreement of Bülow, his staff and Hentsch that unless the gap between First and Second Armies could be closed, a task for which the re-serves did not exist, the two armies would have to retreat, first con-centrically, then conjoined, beyond the Marne. On the following morning, when a review of the situation re-vealed no improvement, Bülow de-cided that Hentsch must go to Kluck and initiate the retreat. So he did.

On his return to OHL, orders were drafted instructing each of the armies to yield its present position and fall back to others more readily defensible: the First to the River Aisne, which it had crossed on 1st September, the Second and Third to the Vesle, one of the Aisne's tributaries, the Fourth towards the line Reims-Verdun, the Fifth to the Argonne and the Sixth towards the border of Lorraine.

They broke contact almost every-where without difficulty for the

**Exhausted German soldiers of the 53rd
Regiment digging in after the Battle of
the Marne**

French and British were not only
exhausted by the retreat and the
battle but quite unprepared for so
sharp and sudden a reversal of German
strategy. When they began to follow
they did so at first cautiously, but as
the first day of advance was followed
by a second, euphoria came to replace
incredulity. General Henry Wilson,
French's Deputy Chief of Staff, spoke
of being at Elsenborn, a German detraining point on the border with
Belgium, in three weeks. Judgements
of this sort were to be proved miser-
ably optimistic. Within three days of
the German retreat beginning, reports began to arrive at GQG of
contact being made with the enemy
in entrenched positions from which he
could not be dislodged. By 17th
September it was clear that the whole
German line, from Soissons on the

Aisne to the Swiss frontier, had been stabilised and was being fortified at a rapid pace. Only on the flank between the Aisne and the sea, on which as yet no operations had taken place, did conditions still exist for mobile operations.

Those operations were to begin at once and to be carried on with desperate intensity throughout the rest of September, the whole of October and the beginning of November, each stage narrowing the area in which armies could operate freely until, by mid-November, not a yard of line on the western front was not defended by earthworks. Traced on a map, the entrenched front described a great reversed S. Ironically its lower loop coincided almost exactly with that Schlieffen had drawn ten years earlier to indicate the line which the German armies were to have achieved on the 33rd day from mobilisation, and from which they would advance to annihilate the French armies.

Bibliography

The Campaign of the Marne Sewell Tyng (OUP, London, 1935)
The Schlieffen Plan Gerhard Ritter (Wolff, London)
France and Flanders 1914 British Official History Vol I (HMSO, London)
The Advance from Mons Walter Bloem (Peter Davies, London)
History of the First World War, Vol I Barrie Pitt (ed) (Purnell, London)
The Origins of the First World War L Albertini (OUP, London)